# The Roadie Wife
## A MEMOIR

*by Bethany Luchetta*

Copyright © 2022
**5 Two Press**
A Nevada Company
ISBN: 979-8-9870276-0-8
2nd Printing

Copyright © 2021
**Bethany Luchetta**
Amazon Publishing
ISBN: 9798453651399
1st Printing

Cover Photo San Francisco, Bay & Taylor Trolley Stop
Cover photo credit: Bethany Luchetta

© Cover Design by Pink Olive Design **www.pinkolivedesign.com**

## Dedication

For Tina Kain & Andrew Kain.
May you forever know my love.

# Chapters

1. VINCE
2. DAVID
3. FEBRUARY 2010
4. DON'T LOOK BACK
5. MARCH 2010
6. JUNE 2010
7. KIDS
8. JULY 2010
9. AUGUST 2010
10. GOING OFF TRACK
11. FILLING VOIDS
12. FALSE HOPE
13. SEPTEMBER 2010
14. VOWS
15. OCTOBER 2010
16. JANUARY 2011
17. FEBRUARY 2011
18. OUT OF PLACE
19. INCOGNITO
20. MARCH 2011
21. APRIL 2011
22. CRUISIN' ALONG
23. SUN AND MOON

24. SUMMERTIME
25. BEHIND THE SCENES
26. AUGUST 2011
27. HIGH ROLLIN'
28. MOONSHINE
29. TABLE DANCING
30. OCTOBER 2011
31. DELICATE THINGS
32. MOVING PIECES
33. CHANGING WEATHER
34. ARRIVING STRESS
35. PERMANENT THINGS
36. JUNE 2012
37. THE ACHE
38. THE BREAK
39. BOTTOM OF THE BARREL
40. PACK IT UP
41. HOMECOMING
42. THE PROPOSAL
43. RECKONING
44. TORONTO
45. FINDING SUPPORT
46. HAWAII
47. MEMORY LANE
48. OCTOBER 2012

"Becoming aware of our behavior is often a springboard into looking at patterns and issues within ourselves; these patterns are a rich source for personal change and improvement."

**Dr. Henry Cloud**

*Chapter 1*

# VINCE

When I met Vince on Halloween of 2009, we were drawn to each other right away. It had been three years since my divorce from David, but Vince and his wife were freshly separated. Vince and I were love-drunk. It was one of those, fall-fast-and-hard stories. We talked of deep things and he was so kind and thoughtful. He made me laugh. He was a sound engineer, traveling in tour buses around the nation with rock stars. We spent every day together for the first two-weeks after we met, until he left for tour.

For the first time since David, I felt like I could let down my guard a little. I felt connected to Vince at a soul level, but no matter how much I felt for him, I couldn't convince my feelings to stop loving David. Afterall, David was my first love. David had played the bass guitar and was roaming the globe as a guitar tech. I think Vince's roadie life was attractive in the same way David's life was: I took pride in being one of those independent, stable types, who could pair well with the roadie life. Even though I wanted a man, I didn't need one. At least that's what I always told myself. It was a convergence of emotion.

I explained to Vince in those early dating days how I had always hoped David and I would get back together at some point and how David and I remained friends through our split. Since we had stayed friends, David was actually with me the day I met Vince. David had agreed to help me with an event I was planning, and that is where I met Vince. After our divorce, I used to ask David to meet the guys I dated, and oddly enough he would indulge me. I am sure it was something sick inside me that either wanted him to be jealous, or that needed his approval.

David was a huge part of my life for so long, and we didn't hate each other, we simply grew apart and didn't know how to keep our marriage together. Of course, we hurt each other in dumb ways spouses do when we are broken and angry, but we still very much cared for each other.

My parents had become very protective after the heartache they witnessed with David, not to mention the handful of jerks I brought home post-divorce. I kept attracting the same non-committal type, and according to my mom, Vince would be no different. The way I saw it, Vince had little chance at winning my parents approval. My mom especially hated that Vince was still getting divorced, and had two daughters along for the ride. Too much, too soon; red flags.

In recounting the memories, my parents had also tried to detour me from marrying David. Had my parents been right about my marriage to David? Should I heed more of their advice about Vince? After all, my first marriage ended as they predicted.

After the divorce, I told David that we could get back together if our relationship could go back to the way it was before it went sour. Were those reconnecting attempts for me, or to make my parents wrong? Relationships can't go back in time like that, "the way things used to be". It was an impossible request. I would know, I tried.

I was falling hard for Vince and I hoped he would take away the desire I had for David. No matter how hard I tried, David was on my train of thought. Maybe I could jump track and go a new direction. Some relationships are mutually exclusive, and that's what I hoped for my feelings; but feelings don't always agree. Something in me still wanted to go back to how I felt before divorce did its dirty deed on my young and innocent heart.

In an attempt to be honest, I tried explaining my converging feelings to Vince. I was confused and my heart was broken. Even though I loved Vince, and wanted to move forward with him, I needed him to know that I mourned for the former "David and Bethany". But, like many young relationships, David and I grew apart, and we did not want the same things anymore.

Chapter 2

# DAVID

David, as I said, was my first love: my high school sweetheart and first (and only) boyfriend. We were inseparable and spent endless days driving around in my car, footloose and fancy free. Seventeen! We even worked for the same company and volunteered in the church youth group together. It wasn't long before we were known as, "Bethany and David". He was funny and charming, and it was often said, the party started when David showed up. We went steady without a breakup, and were engaged in 1999, when I was 19-years-old.

David proposed on a park bench in a neighborhood park down the road from my childhood home. It was simple, sweet and very heartfelt. I rushed home to announce my engagement and show-off *my* diamond. My older sister, Heather, and my mom were sitting at the dining table, doing who knows what. But, I had a diamond on! I flashed that puppy out there in pure unadulterated joy.

To my dismay, joy did not resound at that table. Maybe the acoustics were off in the room? Maybe it was the tile floors?

I could make up a thousand reasons, if I could make up one. I instantly felt shame.

Was I doing something wrong?

I was happy, why weren't they?

They seemed concerned.

I smiled through my pain at their lack of response and pretended like I didn't care what they thought. I was going to get married, and that was that.

My parents objected to my wedding. I rebelled again their objection. As a might-have-been-attorney himself, my dad would say, "a smart industrious young lady should find a doctor or lawyer to marry".

My parents offered opinions about my age, poor matching skills, and immaturity. I rolled my eyes. Their stance (and my rebel stubbornness), inadvertently connected me to David all-the-more.

My parents agreed they would attend my wedding and "support" it if I could agree to their one rule. I had to graduate college before the wedding. Knowing I had two years left to complete my undergraduate degree, I surmised they figured two years' time would slow me down and I would rethink the whole shindig. I agreed to their contest. But instead of slowing down, I doubled-up on coursework while David and I began planning our move to Sydney Australia, aimed for the day after our wedding.

David had planned to attend Hillsong College in Sydney Australia and didn't want to take the journey without me, so we married in January of 2001 and flew to Australia the next day. We managed to rent a small house, subletting rooms to college students to make ends meet while he went to college. I worked days in an accounting department at a janitorial company, and he worked evenings as a server. After a while, David and I were like ships passing in the night, so I quit my job and took a job at the restaurant, where he worked as a server. This helped our time together, we could at least see each other at work. From that time on, I spent my free time volunteering at the church and cleaning houses for extra cash while he was in class.

We worked at Outback Steakhouse, and we both liked it. David actually had high-record sales on a shiny gold plaque near the bar (the plaque may still be there). A lot of people do not know this, but Outback Steakhouse is actually an American Restaurant, designed after an Australia theme. David and I worked at the first Australian location upon their opening year. A lot of other students from David's college worked there too, so it was a fun place to work.

David had been playing bass on the Hillsong United team while attending college with several other band members. After work, students and servers, and band members would congregate at our house for evening bonfires. Our house was built on a rock, literally. Our entire front yard was a massive rock with a shear side where they cut down to build the house. We would have bonfires directly on the rock in the yard and people would stay into all hours of the night.

## The Roadie Wife

It was tough being young, freshly married and away from family, friends and all that was familiar: streets, church, doctors, hairdressers, driving on the proper side of the road! After fourteen months of being in Sydney, David's student visa was up for renewal. So, we analyzed his grades and he got serious about his desire to continue college. Since he wasn't earning passing grades in his courses, and was deciding he didn't really like college after all, we chose to move back to San Diego, California and not renew his student visa. The only problem was that we did not have enough money to get back to California.

Sometimes when David played bass in the band I would go with him, other times I had to work the restaurant. One evening in particular, after we decided we would move back to San Diego, he was scheduled to play an event and I was scheduled to work. He got home before I did and I came in tired and stressed, from trying to figure out ways to get money for the move back home, when David was sitting on our bed with piles of money around him.

I freaked out! My first thoughts were that he robbed someone...or a shop. He's gone crazy. I am going to call the police.

When he saw my look of concern, he blurted, "It's not stolen!"

I breathed a sigh of relief and he began to tell me about what happened at the event. One of the speakers felt someone in the group needed financial help. That someone was David. So, he asked David to come up to the front of the crowd. Since David had just finished playing bass, he rejoined the guy on the stage.

"If you want to give David money, just come up and give it to him." The man announced.

People just started walking up and handing David money. It sounded ludicrous... it sounded miraculous!

After calculating all the cash, we just needed to sell our car to have enough money for our airfare back to San Diego.

We provided notice to our landlord.

Sold our car.

Bought airplane tickets.

And within a few weeks we were packed and ready to go.

It seemed strange that just fourteen months prior we had shipped a household of belongings in a sea container, and now we were leaving with what could fit in our suitcases. What we cherished, and could not fit in our suitcase, we left behind with our trusted friend, Naomi Croker. It wasn't until three years later that I was able to get back to retrieve the rest of our personal items.

# The Roadie Wife

*Chapter 3*

# FEBRUARY 2010

Months into passionately dating Vince, I was driving eastbound on Ninth Avenue, a main thoroughfare through Escondido, California which changes street names four times from start to finish. Ninth Avenue crosses into the next town, over and back again like a swirling snake. I am a Real Estate Broker, and had just finished showing a property on the west side of town and was headed from Auto Park Way where it changes into Ninth Avenue into the Escondido barrio. Truth be told, most of Escondido is now barrio, but this particular area used to be "Pill Hill", where all the local doctors lived in large homes overlooking the city.

As I crossed over Centre City Parkway, the dividing line of one gang territory into the next, I saw a homeless man and swore it could have been my ex-husband. In those days I saw his face everywhere. I was convinced I had some sort of psychosis. Yet, as I continued through the intersection, and approached closer, the homeless man could have been David's doppelganger.

"Oh shit" I said aloud, "That *is* David!".

I passed by as he inhaled on his cigarette. He never smoked cigarettes, that I knew about, when we were together. But, having seen him puffing ever since our marital demise, with his slightly feminine way of holding the cigarette, I knew it was him.

I circled around and pulled over on the side of the road. I still wasn't sure what he was doing just standing on the side of the road. This part becomes blurry, because I can't recall if I got out of the car, flashers on to indicate, "don't hit my car", so I could talk to him on the side of the road, or if I stayed in my car, stretching over to look out the window as he bent down at window height to look in at me. I favor the second memory for some reason, as I don't think I would have gotten out of my car.

"What are you doing?" I asked.

"Oh hey! Just waiting for them to cut me a check." He said, in a casual response.

"Who?" In confusion.

"The temp agency." He answered.

He said it in his typical, sarcastic tone, elevated eye-brows and a half smirk, as he pointed behind him, while holding his cigarette, to their sign on the small building.

"How are you? Why are you in Escondido? Kinda far for a temp agency." I rambled off.

David lived out on the coast now with the Puda brothers, one of which had 301 tattooed on his leg.

"Shit yeah. But you go where they send you." He countered.

"Do you need anything?" I asked.

Why did I ask? Would I have obliged to help if he said yes? Maybe? My track record would say yes, but the new Bethany I was trying to be, would say no. But even still, old habits die hard.

"Nah, I'm goooood. I have my bike." He thankfully said, avoiding my conundrum.

"Ok... Well good seeing you." I said awkwardly, like we were acquaintants.

I paused. I wanted to say, "I love you" or "let's go get some coffee". I wanted to hug him. Maybe this is why I recall not getting out of the car: for fear of smelling him, or hugging too long in the cushion of his flannel coat, or crying on the side of the road with a homeless looking man. Maybe I did get out, and my mind made a new memory that seemed more appropriate for who I was trying to become.

My pause for contemplation must have been too long because I looked up to see him flashing a waiting, half smile, accompanied with an all-too-familiar look. The look peppered with regret and seasoned with recollection of good times. But, this time, the smile was polished with a new whiff of grief. It broke my heart.

I mustered,

"Okay. Bye." And drove off.

# The Roadie Wife

Chapter 4

# DON'T LOOK BACK

Without the slightest change in my stoic face, tears began to stream down my cheeks. As I faced forward, I never looked back, or peered into the mirrors toward the temp agency. I drove to my office on auto pilot and reminisced of the time David called me a few years into our divorce. I was still living at my parents, and it was a scene I replayed often because I was trying to figure out what-might-have-been if I made a different choice that night:

David called and I was already in bed. As a recluse in my quarters, mourning my divorce, I would sleep-in, work, venture back to my room, and slide into bed. I don't recall if the hour was late, or I was just in bed already. I do recall staring at the knotty slats of wood over the top of my bed, mesmerized by their patterns as I answered the phone.

He always started his conversations in a low key, no-big-deal, type of way and occasionally amused himself with a hipster drawl on certain letters. I told him I was in bed.

"Oh shiiiiiit." Was his monotone reply.

He didn't elevate his syllables in a tone of surprise, but just as a point of conversation in the way he says shiiiit, as a common reply, or space holder.

Truth be told, he was in bed too. But only because he was in his tent, and it was his bed, and his house. At this point he was without home, a proper one, living in a tent in his friends' backyard in Cardiff, California. He was a gypsy soul when we were married and now he was free to come and go as he pleased without breaking a lease, leaving a job - or wife. Seemingly, all commitments made him uneasy.

Just a few years prior to David touring, we were freshly divorced and working at another restaurant together, Uno's Chicago Bar & Grill, as part time servers. I had been building my real estate career, and he was trying to keep a job that wasn't piece work. One day serving tables, David got a call from our mutual friend, Michael Chislett, offering David a job as his guitar tech for his band, The Academy Is... (yes, there are ellipsis after the band name).

David and I had met Michael during our first year married in Sydney, when David played bass with Michael in Hillsong United. We had stayed friends with Michael over the years. He would even occasionally stay with us when traveling through the United States and needed a place to stay.

As much as I loved working with David at Uno's, I encouraged him to take the gig with Michael and follow his heart to the road. Maybe leaving would help the two of us emotionally "let go".

After about a year with The Academy Is..., David got offered another gig with the band, Armor for Sleep. He was living his dream, traveling the world with bands, albeit not playing in the band himself. He had just been on a European Tour in the United Kingdom with Armor for Sleep, and wanted to tell me about his journey.

David phoned me from his tent to recap a London rooftop sunset. He was trying to capture it with his words and explaining how I should have been there. It was one of those views where a photo couldn't capture the beauty. His story was too reminiscent of John Mayer's "3x5" song not to sing the lyrics aloud,

"You should have seen that sunrise, with your own eyes. It brought me back to life." I let the lyrics drop from my mouth, then I fell silent.

In my silence, I mouthed the next part of the song. "You'll be with *me* next time I go outside. No more 3x5's". I thought on each word while trying to comprehend what this all meant to me in that moment. I was sucked under the covers trying to hide my vulnerable soul.

He must have felt the same emotion. Maybe already did and that's why he called. He proceeded to invite me over. He missed me. I considered taking this offer because I wanted to be back together so desperately.

I had to reconcile what it would mean to be laying on the ground, with only a thin layer of material between me and the dirt. Where would it go? Would things ever change.

    Not a campground.
    Not a kid playing pretend.
    Just to be with David.
    For love... or for insanity.
    Why did it sound so appealing?

I struggled to decline the invite. I became teary thinking, if "home is where the heart is", wasn't I homeless too?

*Chapter 5*

# MARCH 2010

    A few weeks after I saw "homeless" David on the side of the road, I called him to come for a visit to my new condo. He hadn't seen it yet and it would be nice to show him I was doing okay, and I wanted to talk to him about Vince.
    He always obliged me, even in my most bizarre post-divorce-requests, like meeting the guys I was dating, or taking me on a fancy date. One time I asked him to go out, but he needed to wear something less "homeless" looking, so I bought him a new outfit and played pretend for a fun evening in the San Diego Downtown Gaslamp District.
    This invite to my condo though, was not about pretending. We sat on the back patio of my condo, it had not been ours. I bought it as a "divorced woman", as my title so ineloquently indicated (I felt like the title was mocking me in legal print). It was now four years after our divorce and it took everything to muster courage to tell David about how serious things were with Vince.
    Vince was not just a fling, or a rebound I ensnared to make the senselessness seem *less*

confusing. No, this was Vince: my new soulmate. I felt like I needed to have David's permission, like a dad, but one I would have indulged and not rebelled against.

I wanted him to say, "I can't be what you need Bethany so please take this opportunity for happiness". But, I didn't want him to *mean* it.

I felt like it was the kind of permission someone would need from a deceased spouse to love again. The kind you needed, and really wanted, but didn't want, because you just wanted them back. David wasn't dead though. He was there. But I still couldn't have him back.

The patio tile was cold underfoot as we sat across from one another. He leaned forward with his elbows on his knees, hands together with fingers interlocked. David was sewn into his ever so soft and cushiony, signature flannel coat.

Small talk ensued with passing looks that are hard to forget. We had been friends since we were thirteen and kindly tip-toed through our divorce without ever uttering an ugly word to, or about, one another.

We loved each other too much for bitterness. We just couldn't figure out how to keep the seams from splitting as they pulled in opposite directions of our divergent journeys.

He did end up giving me his full permission to love Vince. But, it felt grief-stricken because we were really moving on. I took his sentiments at face value. I needed to. Then, I had to look away because I could see behind his eyes.

His eyes held a sorrow for what might have been if we could have been more flexible...

More mature...

More of something we just couldn't figure out.

I knew the look.

It was mine too.

Sitting on the patio, we fell silent in loss; loss of words, and one another. David broke the silence in true David form, cutting through the emotional fog.

"Justin Puda lived here, you know?" He said.

David was living with Justin Puda, a former mutual friend of ours, who had re-entered David's life as a band photographer when David and I were splitting up. We had met Justin many years before when David and I were church group leaders and holding youth concerts. Justin, and his brother, Brandon, were now David's closest compadres.

"In this complex?" I queried.

"Nope. This condo." He said.

Pointing to the tile under our feet.

"My condo?" I became more emphatic.

"Yep, before you bought it. Number 301"

He broke up the number in a slow sarcastic rhythmic cadence.

"That's crazy! This was a foreclose when I bought it." I replied.

I was reeling in the crazy coincidence.

"Makes sense. He rented it with 12 other people sprawled all over the place. Crazy things happened here! So crazy, to make sure he never repeated times like that, he tattooed 301 on this leg." David said.

"Holy balls! That's insane." I retorted.
"The place cleaned up pretty good." He said.
He looked around the patio with approval.
"Thanks. I've put some work into it over the last year." In confidence.
I shook my head, with a half-smirk, in wonderment.
"I can't wait to tell Justin." David finished.

Shortly after our patio meeting at my condo, David called to tell me he was moving to Oregon. As he talked, I looked on the patio where we had sat together and it saddened me as I listened to him explain his out-of-state move. I felt like he was growing further away from me. David's father lived in Oregon with his step-mom, half-brothers, and sister. David never stayed close with with his Oregon family after moving to his moms' house in California when he was seventeen. I was glad for his chance to connect with them, as he had always wanted.

Was his move correlated with my relationship with Vince, or pure coincidence? I will never know. Nonetheless, it felt like David was making every effort to move on, as it appeared, I was doing.

I decided it was time to attempt really letting go.

...One can dream.

*Chapter 6*

# JUNE 2010

      Road life attracts interesting types of people. David was one of those; the gypsy soul who doesn't want to be held down. I suppose the gypsy soul sometimes gets preoccupied with the more stationary type, like myself. When David married me, he never let go of his rambling roots. Vince was one of these gypsy souls too. As a touring sound engineer, Vince would live and work on the road, mixing sound for rock stars, in towns all over the North American continent. Maybe there is something of this vagabond spirit which is *actually* attracted to my type. This is my professional opinion (wink).
      Good.
      Bad.
      Indifferent.

      Perhaps I should flip my professional opinion: the stationary types are attracted to the adventurous, whimsical types who will show them a good time. Like much of our life journey, we can't see it while we are in it, so I wouldn't know much about any of this until later.

Vince was still going through his divorce. He and his wife had two daughters, and it was fast approaching their summer visitation with their dad. I had met his girls once before, and truthfully, I hadn't felt ready to meet them when I did. Vince had done the responsible thing and told his ex that he was seriously dating someone, in case the kids would need an introduction at some point. He told her this to be kind and clear, but then she told their daughters. One thing led to another, and his daughters were asking to meet me.

I always felt if I dated a man with kids, I would meet the kids once I was fairly sure I wanted to be with their dad long term. I didn't want to confuse the kids by meeting them prematurely. For me, this meeting was premature. Vince and I were dating less than three months when I first met his daughters.

Because Vince was touring much of the time, it felt like we were still getting to know each other, yet at the same time, our relationship seemed to be moving so fast. He started staying at my condo when he was in town (why not since he was only in town every now and then). My roommate, and best friend, Victoria, had even moved back to her parents to give wide berth for my growing relationship with Vince.

On tour, and then with me when he was home, Vince never seemed to be at his own condo, so he decided to sublease space in his condo. He didn't want to necessarily give up the lease though, you know, in case things didn't work out with me. But, in a random series of events, his sub-lessee, sub-let to two other people. Vince didn't know how to get them all out of his condo in time for summer visitation. He couldn't put his girls in the condo with this sub-lessee and the two squatters.

Being smitten, and so brilliant (sarcasm), I suggested that Vince use my condo for the visitation. I could go stay with my best friend, Victoria, at her parents. Then, Vince and the girls could have my condo all to themselves. This was indeed the quickest way to solve the visitation issue, so he took my offer.

I got so excited to make their visitation special in my condo that I had the girl's names embroidered on towels of their favorite colors: green and pink, and hung them in the guest bathroom. I even put girly touches in my guestroom in attempts at making it more comfortable for them. I told Vince he could use my car to drive up to Northern California to pick up the girls too.

"My Corolla gets better gas mileage than your lifted truck anyway" I rationalized.

I didn't ask Vince what he planned to tell his kids about the car, his condo and my condo, but kids are smart. I am sure they saw between the lines of where our relationship was headed (even if we hadn't yet).

## The Roadie Wife

## Chapter 7

# KIDS

Vince was unveiling another plan during this time, and even though I had only spent a sum total of ten-to-fifteen hours with his daughters, he asked if I would fly them out to see his parents in Boston at the end of visitation. Vince had their visitation timed so that when it was over, he would head back on tour with Jimmy Buffet. His daughters would either return to their mother, or I would agree to his alternative travel plans. Jimmy Buffett was only playing four gigs in June, as part of the Big Top Tour, and two of those gigs were back-to-back shows in Massachusetts, where his parents lived at the time.

His plan would be to fly out for tour rehearsals, and the girls and I would fly out the next day. We would spend the few days at his parents and he could join us for family time. After the short trip, I would fly them home to their mom. It sounded ludicrous, but I consented. His ex would also have to agree to the plan. She did. This would give the kids a chance to see their grandparents, who they hardly ever saw.

Vince left me with his daughters on his pre-arranged travel assignment. He flew out and the next day the girls and I headed down to the airport. We had a red eye flight across the states from San Diego, California to Boston, Massachusetts. The red eye flight was either going to be a good idea if the girls slept, or an awful idea if they didn't. I was hoping we would all sleep on the flight and be rested when we arrived the next day, capitalizing on time with their grandparents.

We approached the airport, found long term parking, and jumped on the shuttle bus toward the Delta terminal. As we walked up I immediately saw on the monitors our plane was *DELAYED* in red. This didn't look promising. After discussing with the clerk, she declared that the plane would not be leaving at all. The fog was not lifting. I smiled brightly trying to hide any worry in my eyes. I turned back to see the girls playing in the nearly empty terminal.

"I have two kids with me. It's late. What do you suggest I do?" I inquired.

"I'll see what we can do for you." She said kindly.

I waited while she clicked away at her computer keyboard.

I explained to the girls that we were on an adventure and tonight that adventure may not be taking flight. I stayed optimistic.

The clerk called me back over. She handed me meal vouchers for breakfast, a free hotel room across the road, and details on our morning flight to Boston.

I hesitated calling the girls' mother, and wondered if that was even my duty. I opted that it was not my duty, and called Vince instead. His voice was composed, but inquisitive about my state of mind. I actually surprised myself. I was being cool and calm. *After all*, I wasn't so good with kids... or animals (a joke I used to say about myself which Vince awkwardly told his kids when I first met them - grimace). But, I was doing my best. Once I was off the phone with Vince, I began to unravel the whole new adventure to the girls.

    We got the hotel shuttle. Surprisingly, and lucky for me, they didn't seem to mind the change one bit! Thank goodness. Little did I know at that time; their entire life was an adventure. They had been moving from place-to-place with their mother and father since they were born. And it didn't seem to get any better for them since their parents split.

    I guess I wasn't as advantaged in quick changes and didn't sleep so well. I was exhausted on our early morning flight out to Boston. Toward the end of the flight I decided I could take a quick snooze if I sat in the end seat, guarding them from the aisle, and they could play secluded in the other two seats against the window. I must have been more tired than I realized, because once I put in my earbuds, I zonked out.

    I woke up needing to use the bathroom. I looked over at the girls, they were playing contently. I took off my seatbelt and motioned to them I was headed to the bathroom. Earbuds still in, I walked to the lavatory as I listened to John Mayer.

Walking to the lavatory, passengers were waving at me and making funny faces. Was there an unspoken rule not to sleep while your kids were awake? Groggy, I found the toilet and shut the door. Once seated, I realized I was leaning... leaning too much. We were *landing*. This was my wake-up call! My eyes widened, as now all the faces and waves suddenly made sense. They were *trying* to get my attention to go back to my seat.

I landed while seated on the lavatory, but not fastened in my 'proper' seat. All I could think of was the girls had to land without me next to them. Then, "oh no, the flight attendants are going to kill me". Before the thought fully registered, I heard a knock on the door. I pulled up my pants and opened the door to the flight attendant in an anger flush.

"What in the world are you doing?" She fumed.

"I am so sorry, I woke up and hadn't even realized we were landing!" I said sheepishly.

"I should write you up with Federal Aviation. Blacklisted to fly with Delta. Ever. Again!" still fuming in anger.

"I am so sorry. I had no idea. I promise. Can you please let me go back to my girls?"

Suddenly they became my children, and I was very protective about getting back to them before they got worried.

"I will let you off with a warning, lady!"

She scowled and moved out of the doorway, directing me with a single pointed finger, back to my seat. I did the walk of shame back to my seat, trying to hold back my laughter at the oddly funny situation.

Chapter 8

# JULY 2010

I had been rationalizing to Vince, even before the Boston trip with his girls and meeting his parents, how my heart still felt attached to David. I couldn't shake my feelings for David. And I was trying to get over David! I was praying I could get over him. Maybe God could just cut the heart strings and I could move on freely. I was doing the best I could to move on into reality.

It seemed like Vince and I had this talk over-and-over; how it felt so challenging to move on with a new relationship. Divorce is hard when the two people hate each other. David and I didn't hate each other, we just sucked at making it work between us. Going through his own divorce, Vince knew this struggle too, and his divorce involved kids, which is more heartbreaking than one without kids.

Divorce showed my human frailty.

It exposed my messiness.

It left me spinning in loss and grief.

It caused me to feel vulnerable.

Feeling vulnerable, I hid: From myself, from the truth, from reality.

I was being truthful with Vince about my still lingering feelings for David. I wasn't all in with Vince - not yet. This message may have conveyed to Vince that I somehow didn't mind if he wasn't all in either. I was trying to be honest and vulnerable, albeit behind my walls. This stuff was so confusing.

But I think we were both dishonest, Vince and me. Dishonest to each other, and ourselves … about our true need to hold each other. I simply didn't know it, or what to do with it.

After several of these high passion, low committal conversations, Vince came home from some one-off gig with Carlos Santana. Carlos had played the Ottawa Bluesfest in Canada where Vince perused the vendor booths finding a beautiful silver ring, appearing to be made with angel dust - glimmer and shine. No diamond. He brought it home in his pocket, entering my room holding the ring with both hands. It was as if he were presenting an item of great worth, between his thumb and pointer fingers. It looked like he was holding a small steering wheel of a miniature car. He began to tell me where he found the ring. I examined it while he was detailing his find.

I loved it. Simple and silver.

"Ottawa, Canada. It stood out on a vendor table." He said.

"It's beautiful! So shiny." I agreed.

He was still holding it while telling me sweet things about life and love.

"It's your size!" He said.

"Yes!" I said.

"Yes?" reconfirming or inquiring.

"I *will* marry you!" I said, excitedly!

We kissed and fell on the bed in sweet embrace. It was blissful.

He went with it.

He later told me that he had not been asking for my hand in marriage that afternoon. My eyes were widened in confusion as my mind was reeling to reenact the events of "the asking", all the while realizing, he indeed, never asked *me,* to marry *him*!

"You should have clarified!" I snapped.

I felt stupid. Jabbing back quickly, without a breath: This is not our first rodeo! We are adults! Who in the world presents a ring like that?!

Can you imagine his thoughts in those moments as I put the ring on?

Had I even put it on myself?

Or did he put it on me?

And then passionately kissing on the bed!?

What must have been passing through his head?!

Who had messed that up?

Quite easily, either of us.

Presumption?

Passivity?

One thing was for sure. It was the foretelling of more to come.

# The Roadie Wife

*Chapter 9*

# AUGUST 2010

Jimmy Buffet tour took a short break in July when Vince was out with Carlos Santana. But, Jimmy Buffet was back on tour in August and Vince asked that I join him on tour when they rolled through Philadelphia, Pennsylvania. Vince grew up in Doylestown, Pennsylvania, near Philadelphia. My dad was born in Upper Darby, Pennsylvania, and my grandpa used to tell me fond memories of eating hoagies on South Street.

When Vince met my grandpa, they bonded right away over stories and places they knew around Philly. It felt comfortable that Vince shared similar Italian heritage and geography.

Vince nicknamed my grandpa, Paisano. They shared the same Italian history, but my grandpa was not biological to me, so I wasn't Italian. Nonetheless, I was raised with Paisano as the only grandpa I knew, loved him dearly, and appreciated that he connected with Vince. Vince romantically figured it would be an awesome adventure to explore South Street together just after being engaged (even if the engagement was only by accident).

I immediately felt a connection to the Philadelphia area, if only by stories, and although I was more interested in seeing Vince, I couldn't help but soak up the history of the area too.

Jimmy Buffett was playing Camden's Susquehanna Bank Center for two shows, with one day off between shows. That put us in the area for three days, which is lucky to come by in the touring industry. Philadelphia is beautiful in the historic parts. But, Camden, New Jersey just across the river is pretty run down in general (even if they do have a Rita's Water-Ice Shop down the road from the arena).

The Susquehanna Arena is right on the Delaware River looking directly across toward downtown Philly. The arena may be Camden's only claim-to-fame, and lucky for them, because major tours stop there bringing them tourist business.

The entire venue parking lot was taken over for three days with Jimmy Buffet fans, self-titled as, "Parrot Heads" - some who don't even go home for those entire three days. Parrot Heads are known for bringing boats and other recreational vehicles to the venue parking lot to create a faux island paradise.

The parking lot becomes a huge tail-gate party called, Margaritaville. Margaritaville is basically a middle-age frat party. Even though Parrot Heads are a mix of all ages, most are middle-aged business people who trade in their suits for island wear, briefcases for feathers, and coffee cups for shots of tequila.

Some fans have so much fun in Margaritaville, that they never make it inside the venue for a single song. I wasn't into the island paradise theme, so I steered clear of Margaritaville, and the Parrot Heads.

Michael Chislett, the longtime friend of David and mine from Sydney Australia, was playing with his band, The Academy Is... and it happened, they were the opening band for K.I.S.S, at the Susquehanna the night before Jimmy Buffet's show. I always find it strange how you can travel the whole world around and still run into the same people by chance. The evening I arrived in Philadelphia, Vince and I met Michael in Chinatown for some Pho, and caught a bit of Michaels show before his tour headed out of town.

Seeing Michael reminded me of the 'good old days' when David and I met him back in Sydney. Michael was a few years younger than me, and he had only been out of high school for a short time when David and I moved to Sydney. Michael and his wife had only started dating when we met them. I was happy our friendships stood the test of time, even after my divorce. Especially since David had been Michaels guitar tech before switching over to Armor for Sleep.

The following day Vince and I hit the streets snapping photos along the way for my Paisano back in California. My grandpa loved *love,* in his old age. He was known for being spiteful and mean in his younger years; an only child spoiled by his mother. But, he was changing and Paisano loved that I had found myself an Italian from Pennsylvania, and I kind of loved it too.

I documented everything I could of my trip, from Jim's on South Street, to the Liberty Bell and Independence Hall. I could share it all with Paisano when I returned. It was nice thinking about being married again, hand holding through the city, all-the-while trying to find my way out of love with David, even if he seemed to loom just below the surface of everything. Having dinner with Michael of course reminded me of old times, but now old times seemed to be merging with new ones.

To celebrate our engagement, Vince found a restaurant called, Buddakan, just down the street from our hotel. It was along Chestnut Street which led down to Penn Landing at the Delaware River, directly across from Susquehanna venue. It was Asian fusion cuisine, elegantly lit with candlelight, small tables, and above the bar was a huge golden buddha surrounded by a red velvet curtain.

We ordered unfiltered Nigori and began searching the menu for our choice of appetizers and main dish items to share. I wore a pink and white striped summer dress with spaghetti straps. If you know me, wearing a dress is rare. So, this night was special. I felt as graceful as the restaurant, albeit, not as ritzy. After dinner we walked down toward some nightclubs and martini bars. We saw Robert, an engineer for Jimmy Buffet, walking with his girlfriend, Wanda, and asked them to join us. We spent the remainder of the evening talking about our ex's and listening to the guys tell roadie stories.

*Chapter 10*

# GOING OFF TRACK

It was tough moving into a new marriage while contemplating how the last one ended. I suppose that's good to an extent – learn from your past mistakes. For my sake, or the pressure of society, when David and I were married, he was always trying to conform to my version of a stationary lifestyle (even if he was bursting at the seams to break the mold). For that reason, and my then unknown internal drive, we moved more than other couples, and we could never decide if we should have children.

We lived in seven different houses in our five years of marriage. In 2005, we lived on Archwood Street. This was our house before we separated in early 2006. Archwood Street has sorrow in its walls from our months of relational combat. As we tucked behind trenches, defenses were being erected; we were lost in a war with no armistice in sight.

I didn't know back then how and where my pain originated, but I knew there was an emptiness inside me, and David too. It was a pervasive longing that neither one of us knew how to fill. The more we tried to fill the void, the more we seemed to injure one another. We would become frustrated and retreat behind our walls again. It was an overwhelming, hopeless pursuit.

It was during our time at Archwood Street that I attended a few sessions with a psychiatric therapist. David described me as 'erratic' to a 'pill-pushing' doctor who labeled me after one meeting. He sent me away with two scripts: Prozac for depression and Lithium for bi-polar disorder. Not long after taking the medicine I felt robotic and lifeless.

One day I got angry, I had enough of the calculated robotic fog, and flushed all my pills. David was furious that I would deny the doctor's orders. He felt somehow, I was capturing him into a prison of misery, and that I was the main problem in the marriage. He was hoping the pills would fix what was broken between us. I felt misdiagnosed, at a core level, and knew living in a dulled state of mind was not going to fix what was wrong with me. I wanted to take my health on another path. I just couldn't seem to find the path I needed.

It wasn't long after the pill flushing that David suggested we try weed. David, and our longtime friend, Josh, along with his wife, talked about the possibility of smoking weed altogether. After a short discussion, it was unanimously decided to try marijuana at an appointed date and time.

Josh and his wife had been in youth group with David and me – by this time we had all been in each other's weddings, and done about ten years of friendship together.

Josh and I were friends from the time we were in elementary school. Our families attended the same church and since he was from a broken family, my mom adopted Josh for holidays, and weekends, and just about any time Josh wanted to come over. Josh even joked that if my sisters and I all married, he would have to marry our Nana to get into our family.

Josh and I met David because David's mom was a church friend of my mom. David had been kicked out of high school in Oregon for bringing weed to school, so when David moved to town from Oregon to live with his mom, he attended our church too. Josh and I had been fairly behaved teenagers growing up, and Josh took a fondness to David's rough side. David was a few years older than Josh, but one night shortly after they met, Josh unequivocally asked David,

"Can we be best friends?" in true elementary school yard fashion.

Sounds silly. But, it worked.

I was tasked with the job of finding weed. I felt like I was sneaking around like a naughty teenager waiting to be caught by my parents. I asked around at work and managed to come up with a bag of weed and met back at our Archwood Street House. I threw down my bag of weed on the coffee table, like a true poser, presenting my job well done to the group.

Turns out I was really the *only* uninformed one in the whole bunch; I was so naïve. It wasn't long before I realized I was the only one who had not smoked weed before, they all had.

I was *so* innocent that I didn't even know you needed some way to smoke it. I now realize it must have been funny for all of them; sending the sheltered girl on a weed hunt. But lo and behold, they knew what we would need, and without hesitation, David grabbed a chair and headed into our master bedroom closet. He hopped up on the chair, removed the attic-lid, and pulled down a homemade weed pipe.

**Aghast.** I didn't know how to feel at first. How long had he been smoking behind my back? Arg.

I wanted to drill him. But, it wasn't the moment for a battery of questions, so I let it slide.

We smoked a bit (I smoked a smidge, I have no idea how much they smoked). I ended up preferring whiskey to weed though. It was summertime and I recall running around my house in my two-piece, homemade bikini: not high, but drunk.

The next day I felt wrong. This wasn't us, "David and Bethany". Recounting the events, and the questions I didn't ask, surrounding that evening, I couldn't shake the feeling that we were on our way to living different lives.

The days and weeks after the marijuana situation at Archwood Street, I found myself wondering where my marriage was going? I went to work every day and David was spending more nights out playing bass with his band. There was a chasm coming between us, and I felt like we were both ready to walk away from the fighting line with a white flag. I could feel it coming.

## Chapter 11

# FILLING VOIDS

When David and I moved back from Sydney in 2002 I got a job at the Escondido Sports Center and Skate Park as the Recreational Coordinator. I coordinated the programing for kid's indoor soccer, roller hockey and the skate park. A group of us shared a small office in the park and ran the facilities. I had a window desk that overlooked the grass area along the road into the parking lot.

Our building was connected to a pro-shop and a concession stand. The City would rent the pro-shop and the concessions to the highest bidder as a way to earn income for the facilities.

Two years into working at the park, the rental contract came up for renewal and SDSF, San Diego Skate Foundation, won the bid for the pro-shop and concession space. *Rumor* in the underbelly-skate-world was the initials actually stood for: Skate. Drink. Smoke. Fuck (I can neither confirm or deny this). But the shop couldn't post that on a sign in a City park. SDSF was owned by 4 professional inline-skaters: Mac, Geoff, Jon and Mattias.

The skate park was famous back in its heyday for being one of the only metal skate parks in North America. We hosted professional skaters like, Bob Burnquist, Tony Hawk and Shaun White. I coordinated professional, and semiprofessional, events for skateboarding, inline skating and extreme BMX bike competitions.

In 2004 the City began plans to demolish, and redesign, the old metal skate park into a new composite park. A main reason the metal park had to go was because metal ramps had to be screwed together. And screws, unscrew, causing trip hazards for skaters. One day, professional inline-skater (and owner of SDSF), Mac, lost his finger when his wedding ring got snagged on a screw from one of the ramps.

I'll never forget poor Sara, who was working the skate park that day.

"Mac came running to the office window with his finger inside the palm of his hand! Yelling to call 911. Blood everywhere!" Sara recounted in horror.

The doctors were not able to reconnect his finger. Mac sued the City. Apropos. His waiver of liability held up in court though, and he lost the case.

By summer of 2005 remodeling began. The famous metal park would be replaced with a new wood composite material, sans screws.

Geoff, one of the pro shop owners, was incredibly attractive and super cool. This didn't help with my marital problems. *And* Geoff and I were both part of the skate park redesigning team, which gave an excuse to spend extra time talking with him after, or during work – even if we weren't exactly talking about skate park business.

Weeks after the marijuana incident, when wondering what was happening in my own marriage, I found myself imagining what life would be like with Geoff instead of David. Would it be better or worse? Would I feel so lonely? My imagination would get the best of me, if I wasn't able to catch it first.

During the slow time of construction, I would find myself in the pro shop with Geoff. Week-after-week I soaked in the attention I was *not* getting at home. Even though I tried to subdue my feelings for Geoff, I noticed an internal excitement to go to work. I would become awe-struck when I saw him drive into the parking lot from my desk window. He was unknowingly filling a slice of my void - and I really liked looking at him (or was it gawking?).

My imagination *was* getting the best of me with Geoff, and I was also hearing a buzz about David and a band groupie. I couldn't prove anything about the groupie at the time, but I felt it was indeed true.

David played bass in a garage band. His band played weekend shows at local bars, and were gaining popularity by the week... and more groupies. Most bass players I know are notorious for their anonymity, which is attractive to the right person, and it wasn't long before that *right* person was attracted to David. It was the attention he should have been getting from me, but wasn't.

My instinct was confirmed about the groupie when some friends showed me some photos on MySpace. She wasn't trying to hide her time with David and had been bragging online about stealing a married man... and I was the wife being stolen from.

David and I were severing down the middle. I was staying late at work to talk with Geoff and David stayed out more with the band and groupies. Arguments of jealousy became a normal routine until they faded into silence and indifference. I guess we got tired. We both sensed this train was headed nowhere for us, but we couldn't stop it from moving with all its momentum.

People need to feel cared for. It's not a flaw. But, trying to fill the need outside of marriage became my flaw. I will never be sure which emotional affair came first. But, it really doesn't matter, I owned my part. David and the groupie, and Geoff and I, are another story altogether (which may, or may not ever be told). But those days served as a lesson, a bittersweet one; like a 301 leg-tattoo, I lesson I never want to forget.

*Chapter 12*

# FALSE HOPE

There was one incident during our time at Archwood Street, in particular, that put a nail in the coffin for David and me. David had just undergone dental surgery for removing his wisdom teeth. It was arduous and he needed some heavy medication. I had planned on attending a skater party that night, but there was no way David was getting out of bed. So, instead of going alone, I called Josh go with me.

Sadly, I was so giddy to get out of the house to see Geoff at the party, I was insensitive to David's pain from the oral surgery. Although David was the only one I ever loved, at this point, I was growing very fond of the extra-marital attention from Geoff. I gave David some prescribed pain killers, his cheeks as chubby as a squirrel, and I walked out. I left him lying in bed alone. He knew. I knew. Flames were fanning and it wasn't for our love. Our bridge was burning.

After months of indifference, David and I lay on the floor at Archwood Street in front of the crackling fireplace and discussed our future. It was warm and the ambiance actually created a cloud of hope for our marriage.

Our conversation had boiled down to two choices: one, have a baby and try to make our marriage work, or two, go back to Australia (where we *thought* we were happy together) and try and make our marriage work. I'm not sure, even in hindsight, what phase we were going through at this point, but we both agreed, we owed it to each other, and ourselves to *try* something.

Maybe change would help? Maybe going back in time could help? After much deliberation, we chose the plan to downsize and started planning a move back to Australia. The next day we put in our 30-day notice to leave Archwood Street and started a search for a small, inexpensive studio to save money for Australia. We were filled with optimism expending energy toward a similar goal. And for the first time in well over a year, we felt united in our marriage.

It didn't take long to find a small one-bedroom apartment with everything we needed. Luckily, we were able to lock-in a month-to-month lease which would give us the ability to save, and jet-set, when we were ready to move back to Sydney.

We sold, or gave away, most of our furniture, except our basics *and* our oversized stainless-steel refrigerator (because we had *just* paid cash for it).

The refrigerator became a sad joke because it looked like an elephant in our tiny studio. Later it was a sore spot and I would end up just giving it away, as it was a memory of the hopeful time we had moving to that tiny studio.

We bought a few marriage books and made a commitment to try to fix what was wrong (had we even known?). Each book was pried open at least to the first or second chapters. As the days and weeks passed, we slowly melded back into old habits and the books faded into the coffee table - forgotten altogether.

We never changed any of our daily routines, so I guess you can't fix a marriage by trying to repair the symptoms. I guess the hope of going back in time can only sustain you for a limited time before reality peeks it's ugly head through your false hopes (things I hadn't known at the time).

A few months later Josh came over to hang out with David. I headed out to hear some jazz music with Geoff and my 'new group' at Pounders, a biker dive bar, in our town. I had never been in Pounders before because it looked so seedy. But this is where the music was, and my new friends.

About an hour into the show, I saw David walking through the crowd, toward another couple. I was confused and watched him walk like he was on a mission. But before he got to them, he looked around the room and we met eyes. I smiled and he changed course to my table.

He pulled me into a quieter area, and told me shortly after I had left, the upstairs neighbor came down and threatened him. The neighbor identified himself as 'Zipper-Face' and was hidden under tattoos, on almost every discernible portion of his body. He had warned David to, 'Keep the noise down *and* stop having parties!'

Later I talked with David about why he had been walking up to the other couple in the bar. He said, he thought it was me with another guy. He felt anger to confront me. But he second-guessed himself, and that is when he looked up and happened to see me across the room. He said, it caused him to think why he cared at all even if I *had* been sneaking around behind his back.

This made me sad because the truth was evident; neither of us would fight for our relationship anymore. This was the downward slope of indifference for me and David. We were playing the married single life. White flags were waving.

Three months later we filed for divorce.

## Chapter 13

# SEPTEMBER 2010

Vince and I enjoyed our time in Philadelphia celebrating our new engagement, then I flew home and Vince continued on the tour. Jimmy Buffet would be taking a three week break after Labor Day. During tour breaks, Vince was home more often. When he was home, he would be assigned one-off gigs, and sometimes be away for a few days at a time.

Being a roadie is like construction piece work. I guess the main difference is he had an employer who contracted him out for shows, instead of being an independent contractor. Basically, he was a sound engineer gigolo who was pimped out by his company.

When Vince wasn't home, his home-away-from-home was a big shiny coach liner where he lived with ten other guys in two rows of bunk beds, three high, on either side of the bus with a hallway down the center leading into the back lounge. The bus had a small kitchen and tiny toilet room, which was exclusively for, 'pee and not poop' (as I was constantly told).

Each bunk had a privacy darkening curtain, as if a curtain made you feel like you actually had any privacy. You could most reasonably reach out and touch the nose of the guy across from you. Every couple of days the crew would get a hotel, real privacy, a poo, a long warm shower, and the ability to fully stretch their legs while sleeping.

Vince was assigned the Epicenter music Festival in Fontana California at the Auto Club Speedway at the end of September. I heard Michael's band, The Academy Is... was going to be playing the event too. My best friend, Victoria, and I figured we should go up: close to home, a cool line-up, I could see Vince, and visit with Michael. Unfortunately, the event was being held on the speedway blacktop and it ended up being 106 degrees. I wasn't sure if Victoria was going to make it for the evening lineup, water was running low on the race track, and she was suffering some heat exhaustion.

Michael took us up to artist catering, out of the sun, to eat, and for Victoria to cool down. Vince and I had just seen Michael in Camden opening for K.I.S.S. before the Jimmy Buffet show. But, since we had seen him, his band had started splitting at the seams. The Academy Is... was coming to an end. He informed us this Epicenter event would be his last show with his band. He had just married Naomi eighteen months before, and was a little uneasy about losing a solid paying gig. Life was changing again for us all: David was gone to Oregon, Vince and I were about to marry, and Michael was leaving his band.

The evening line-up was stacked. Victoria and I stood side-stage to watch a high-school favorite, Blink 182. We also caught performances by 30 Seconds from Mars and Against Me. Eminem was also there, touring again since his musical hiatus, so that was a big deal. The touring music life has some fun perks, and I was enjoying being engaged to a roadie.

Vince's time home went by too fast and he was gone again. We hoped to see each other every three weeks when he was on the road, so I studied the tour calendar to find places to insert myself.

# The Roadie Wife

## Chapter 14

# VOWS

Vince and I must have figured moving fast was the best way to get over former love because we made plans to elope on 10/10/10 over the cliffs of Carlsbad, California. In attendance were our dear friends Victoria, Wendy, and her husband, Jeff. Victoria officiated our ceremony. Vince's divorce was set to be final by the end of September, so 10/10/10 made a great date and eloping made sense because we had both been married before (and we didn't want any fuss – or the opinions of our family to slow us down).

Our planned wedding date was scheduled conveniently so Vince could move into my condo at the end of his lease. Sometime during the summer, we resolved to practice abstinence until our nuptials. At the time, the decision for abstinence came 50 percent from guilt and 50 percent from wanting to set a moral example for Vince's daughters. But, we both knew we couldn't keep holding out forever. Additionally, I thought the date was clever symbolizing the number of 'divine completion' according to biblical texts.

To my dismay, and absolute frustration (the understatement of the decade), his then-wife held up the divorce process when she found out about our plans to marry. She 'conveniently' lost the court paperwork and Vince was informed by the court clerk his divorce was *not* set to be finalized as we had hoped.

Quite impatient, and indignant at the legal requirements, we decided to keep our scheduled cliffside vows for 10/10/10. After all, getting married was a commitment before witnesses, *not* a legal document (that is what I kept telling myself). Since this was an awful example for Vince's daughters, we decided not to tell them the full truth at that time, digging us further into a ditch with the whole story.

To heck with conventional, bureaucratic red tape, and any sort of legal (or moral) requirement. I was set to have my way. His then-wife knew our plans and made jokes that we were sister wives. I just pretended it didn't upset me, and shrugged it off (scowl).

After our Carlsbad cliffside vows, we went to Love Boat Sushi with our three friends, Victoria, Wendy and Jeff, and celebrated as man and wife. Vince's divorce was final in December. And then, as officially required by the county, we had two friends join as obligatory witnesses at the courthouse chambers of the judge to stamp official marriage documents. We were legally married on December 29, 2010, making it the second time we exchanged our vows. However, I never made mention of the true version of this story, and put up our "Established on 10/10/10" plaque at our house.

*Chapter 15*

# OCTOBER 2010

Just after our vows on 10/10/10 was my next trip to visit Vince in Irvine, California. This is when the reality of Vince's job began to rattle this roadie wife.

The October air had a cool bite, so Vince and I unanimously voted to take a dip into the hotel jacuzzi after dinner. I hadn't expected to visit the pool, so I didn't bring my suit. I settled for a t-shirt and Vince's boxer briefs. I wrapped in a towel and followed him barefoot down the red carpeted hall to the elevators.

As we rounded the corner, we saw Robert, walking hand-in-hand with a female. I had met Robert a few months ago in Philadelphia. He was dating Wanda. I almost waved until I notice this female *wasn't* Wanda.

Robert approached his room, releasing the lady's hand long enough to reach out and swipe his room key. He ushered her into his room by the small of her back while glancing back to us, bouncing his eyebrows up-and-down.

I was PISSED. OFF.

Robert had just explained to Vince and I that he was going through a divorce. And even though he was still living with his wife and kids, he emphatically declared: His. Marriage. Was. Over.

So, what was this?

Seething, I began to forcefully drill Vince without a breath - or a chance for him to answer (answering wasn't the point).

Isn't Robert dating *Wanda*?
Is he *really* going through a divorce?
Or was that just a story to tell Wanda?
Who the hell was *that* lady?
Does *she* know he's married *and* dating Wanda?
What the heck do you guys do on the road?
Are you seeing other women?

Truth be told, I was so livid, I let it ruin my evening. I couldn't pull out of my elevated emotions to enjoy my time with Vince. I was too busy wondering what all these gypsy guys do while away from their families. In the jacuzzi, I ceased my rant to sit silently across the from Vince, isolated in my own thoughts.

These are the vagabond types: these are the guys I fall in love with.

It's a matter of fact, when I get that angry, it means something is hurting inside me. I must have hated something in the situation, dangerously close to my own pain. I felt these emotions exposing me, calling me out to pay attention.

I didn't like it one bit – and had no idea why.

*Chapter 16*

# JANUARY 2011

    Jimmy Buffet was off for the remainder of 2010. Vince was back to working local shows or one-off gigs with artists who needed an engineer. His work schedule was busy. To top it off, his family came to town for a visit over the holidays. We had Vince's girls and ventured with his family to Pasadena, California for a few days to see the Rose Bowl Parade. We had just married and it seemed we were both too busy for any time together.

    Vince was home for the holidays, and then gone again. In January (the month after our legal court house nuptials) Vince got assigned Kid Rocks 40th Birthday Bash in Michigan. At that time, the Midwest was experiencing their polar vortex. Vince didn't normally mind the cold, but working outside in below zero temperatures was wrecking his hands. He needs his hands to work. He was miserable.

    Mid-January I got a call from Vince's Human Resource Director. It was the day Vince was flying home from the Kid Rock 40th Birthday Bash.

    "Bethany, it's Shannon. Call me back asap. Vince is landing today, but we have already booked him another flight out. He needs fresh clothes and his plane ticket. Call me and I will get you details."

This was another introduction to roadie wife life of a touring sound engineer. Vince and I had looked forward to a semi-quiet spring, since Jimmy Buffet would be in Europe, which would allow us coupling time while Vince worked locally.

I called Shannon back to discover the other 'official' Kid Rock sound technician had quit. Vince was being rearranged off the Jimmy Buffet tour to the Kid Rock tour. They needed him to turn around and start spring tour. I chuckled. Was this a joke?

"Not a joke." She continued, "He will need a bunch of clothes. His flight takes off this afternoon, after he lands. I will email you his new itinerary."

I would have packed some clothes, but I don't pack for other people. I looked at his landing time and take off time, and decided it was enough for him to pack himself. It would also give us some time together. I began to think; did he even agree to this yet? Does he have a choice? Turns out he didn't have much of a choice. He does work for a pimp – he goes where he's told.

He landed and I was waiting in the terminal. He had already listened to the voicemail from his boss and approached me, with a half smirk, half frown. He knew our newlywed plans of conscious coupling were ruined. I told him that I didn't pack his bag, because he had enough time to pack himself and so we headed home.

Hours later we were back at the airport. We parked. I walked him inside, trying to capitalize on each moment before he left again. He was headed right back to Detroit to start the new tour with Kid Rock and Jamey Johnson. I told him goodbye, and that he will love Jamey Johnson. Up to this point, Vince wasn't much a of country music fan, so I told him to listen really closely to the song "In Color", which was one of my favorite country songs by Jamey Johnson. We kissed and he disappeared into the land of TSA.

    Back at home John Mayer lyrics played throughout the house as I sat alone, reminding me that, "...all we ever do is say goodbye".

#  The Roadie Wife

*Chapter 17*

# FEBRUARY 2011

  Vince and I looked over calendars, time frames, and costs of airline tickets so I could start planning my first trip to see him out on the tour with Kid Rock. It turned out that in two-weeks he would be in Fort Worth, Texas for a few days. Finding a city where they stay for more than two days during a tour, isn't easy with some artists. Kid Rock was one of them and Carlos Santana was worse. I was wishing he was still with Jimmy Buffet, he always had several days in once place. But those days were now in the past.

  I had never been to Texas, and all the way up until the day of the trip, I was excited. But the evening I flew out, a freak snow storm hit Fort Worth. It was also Super Bowl Weekend: Packers vs Steelers at Cowboys Stadium. I don't care for sports, so that didn't faze me. In fact, I didn't even know who was playing until I got into town. I took a midnight flight from San Diego and arrived in Fort Worth around five in the morning.

  I looked outside the airplane window, as we began to land, and saw fields of white. The airport felt shut down; it was quiet and cold. It didn't take long to discover taxis were on strike, which I thought was ludicrous for such a popular weekend. I soon found out most drivers were on strike because of a new law that allowed natural gas taxis to jump the line at the airport, reportedly putting a dent in pocketbooks of all standard gasoline powered taxis.

I sat in the terminal trying to figure out how I would get from the airport to downtown, which was about 25 miles – in the snow – uphill both ways (cheesy smile). I contemplated public transportation or attempting a last-minute rental car. I wasn't going to need a car, so I opted for commuting via public transportation, after all, I was getting better about finding my way around new towns.

Before stepping outside into the cold, I opened my suitcase in a corner, pulled out every piece of clothing I could pile on to keep warm, and set out on my commute.

While I was waiting for the bus outside, it was just me and one other guy. The other guy appeared to be waiting for a ride too. He had his suitcase laid on the ground and was using it as a seat, with his knees almost to his chin.

As I approached this, only-other-human-in-the terminal, near my bus stop, I noticed his strong jaw, squared forehead, low hairline and how he distinctly smoked his cigar.

Holy Hellboy. It's Hellboy! I emphatically declared (but only in my head). I looked around to see if someone else was nearby to confirm my excitement. But, there wasn't, so I just shrugged and acted cool.

I am the only other person waiting for a ride in this taxi-striking, freak-of-snowstorm, Super-Bowl-weekend-airport-terminal with Ron Perlman! I wanted to say, 'Hello Hellboy' just for fun, but I didn't want to be that weird... or awkward. Instead, I just hovered awhile until my bus came, knowing eventually I would write a story about hanging out with Ron Perlman. I guess if I struck up a conversation, this story would have been so much better.

The bus took me from the airport to a nearby train station. The train would take me the rest of the way into downtown by the clock tower. What I didn't know, the train station was out in the open. The open snow. It may have been my first memory of snow fall. As in, snow falling on me while standing outside in the cold. The train finally arrived.

At this time, I received a call from Vince indicating he couldn't wait much longer before heading out to the gig. We had planned on having breakfast and heading to the gig together. I was disappointed, but all I wanted now was a warm bath, food and sleep.

The train slowly traveled down the tracks, rocking back and forth along the snow. I pressed my head against the glass window. The heat from my breath made fog on the window. I pulled back and rubbed my sleeve on the window to clear up my fog. I proceeded to ruminate and steam from the inside about traveling into the cold. I just wanted to be back home with my husband in San Diego! Where it was warm, even in February.

I arrived to the clocktower station, and my luck turned a bit. I wasn't sure how I would get from the station to the hotel, but there were some independent drivers waiting at the station to take travelers to their destinations. Hallelujah!

The driver dropped me off under the Hampton Inn & Suites sign on Commerce street. I no sooner entered the lobby as the hotel doors opened to Vince and the crew emerging. It was the look on their faces that made me question the look on my own. A handful of guys waved goodbye as I grimaced and walked by.

Vince handed me a hotel keycard and told me the room number.

"Order some room service, take a warm bath and a nap, and then let's talk later." He kissed me and headed to the bus.

I just nodded, with an acknowledging look, knowing that is exactly what I wanted - no words were needed - I followed the plan in precise order.

*Chapter 18*

# OUT OF PLACE

I woke up in the hotel bathrobe surrounded by a feather filled comforter feeling much better. I stretched and rolled myself out of bed. Standing to see silver emerging between the curtain opening, I pulled the curtains back and took in the beauty from the fifth-floor hotel bay window. I breathed in the view for a moment before contacting Vince for the gig location. Kid Rock was playing the ESPN Pre Super Bowl Party. I got all the details, and planned to arrive well before the event, so I didn't get lost in the flood of arriving guests.

Upon arriving, Vince met me outside the event tent. He led the way through the snow, flashing his laminate credentials to each security guard, as we went further into the venue. The tent was huge. It was equipped with heaters, ritzy furniture, a full stage and several bars. I met some of Vince's new house/bus mates, and some of the other crew I had known from former gigs. One of them was Robert and to my surprise, beside him was Wanda, who drove up to see him. I took a huge breath upon seeing her, knowing about Robert at the Irvine Hotel. I just wanted to keep to myself. But,

Wanda and I were prompted to 'buddy-up' during the event because the guys would be working and they wanted to make sure we weren't alone.

The crowd began arriving and the tent became very crowded with athletes, actors, musicians, and very glamourous looking people. I did not fit in. I must have felt vulnerable and out of place, because I took this opportunity to soak up my fair share of free peach absolute vodka (okay, truth be told, I drank way more than my fair share). Wanda was pointing out celebrities. I may have flirted with a few, because there were so many to choose from, and why not.

I recall standing next to some sort of athlete, I presume to have been a basketball player because the top of my head was looking at his ribs. My eyes were wide with amazement as I moved my head slowly from his chest to his face. He looked down at me and gave a knowing smile, indicating while nodding, that people my height always give him the same look.

I remember Wanda talking very loud over the sound system about her relationship with Robert and the altercation between his wife and her. Apparently, Roberts wife did not know about Wanda, or the fact he had been claiming his marriage was over. To say the least, it was over now. She felt bad, but not bad enough to end her relationship with Robert. He was now 'staying' at her place for weeks at a time when he wasn't on tour. It wasn't long before the event was over, but I don't remember most of it.

After an event is over, it's a well-known fact in the industry, if people linger too long, they bring up the house lights. Then security begins working the perimeter, starting in the furthest corner, ushering people toward the exit. Much like cattle herding. If you have credentials, you stay, if not, you go. I had Vince as my credentials. I could most reasonably stay past the ushering out of the party guests. But I was in no shape to stay and wait on the crew dismantling gear.

Vince introduced me to Mark, Kid Rocks drum tech, who would escort me out to the tour bus. I hugged Wanda goodbye and reached behind her into the bar and grabbed myself an unopened bottle of peach vodka. I don't think the bartender saw me, but then again, I had more than my fair share. I slid the bottle into my coat and headed for the exit with Mark. I heard chuckles from the crew. But no one ratted me out, so I kept walking as innocently as possible without looking back.

On the bus, Mark asked me tons of questions about Vince. Vince was the new guy on this tour and the crew was still trying to figure out his sarcastic personality. We joked and talked about personalities and road life. Other crew joined us and I gave them a little insight to Vince, maybe some ammo. I was having a great time, joking and getting familiarized with Vince's roadie family.

Mark told me about his new love interest and wanted to show me her photo. He handed me his phone. I was quite inebriated and decided I would swipe and see the next photo on his phone.

The next photo was a naked selfie. He quickly grabbed the phone out of my hand.

"Never swipe... You never swipe!" He exclaimed.

"Nice naked selfie!" I said loudly.

I put emphasis on *'naked'* to attract the attention of the other guys on the bus. The bus broke into laugher, as we mocked Mark by continually saying, 'Never swipe. You never swipe!' It became a joke carried on for months.

The next day the snowy weather began clearing. It was Super Bowl Sunday in Dallas-Fort Worth, Texas. I joined Vince and the crew at the hotel venue where everyone was bustling about preparing for the Super Bowl after party. Kid Rock was scheduled to play the celebration party for the Green Bay Packers.

I have no idea how these things work, but I hear they plan for both teams to win; hats, shirts, parties, even championship rings. Vendors need to be equipped with gear to sell as soon as the game is over. Apparently, someone is in charge of destroying all the gear for whichever team doesn't win. Seems like a waste. But, I guess people want to celebrate the moment the game is over. The stage must be set - after party and all!

I arrived with the crew toting my luggage behind me, because I had to grab a car to the airport before the party started. The crew began setting stage for an elaborate Green Bay Packers Championship evening.

The party had an ice palace theme. In the middle of the room was a ginormous ice sculpture, three times bigger than me. Event crews were covering the walls with silver, angelic-looking curtains. Large bars and buffet tables were being erected across the room.

I must have looked out of place, because every thirty minutes or so a security would ask to see my credentials. I imagined all this was such a consumeristic waste if Green Bay didn't win.

I began contemplating conspiracies, they already knew who would win, and the Steelers didn't actually have a room like this across town somewhere. It was surreal, even for someone who could care less for sports. VIP's do things with an air of pretention that seems so illusionary. I felt the abnormality of it. It wasn't my daily reality, but I did have one foot in this wild world because I was a roadie wife.

# The Roadie Wife

## Chapter 19

# INCOGNITO

I found my next spot on Vince's calendar, but this time I wanted to surprise him, so I didn't tell him about my plan. I had a three-day weekend for Presidents' Day and figured I could capitalize on time with Vince for his day off. I scheduled a flight into Raleigh, North Carolina, the evening before the tour buses made it to town. I rented a car, and found a decent hotel. I called Vince on my way to my solo dinner in Raleigh and conjured-up a story about taking myself out to eat, albeit in San Diego.

It was kind of fun being incognito. Then I realized how easy it was to trick someone, and felt a little uneasy about the whole thing.

The next day I arrived at the hotel where the tour was staying, and peeked about to see if Vince was walking around anywhere. I ran into some crew, who were surprised to see me. They informed me that Vince hadn't made it into the room and was still asleep in his bunk.

I got the bus code and snuck my way into the beds, careful not to wake any other sleepers. I creeped up to his top bunk and touched him through the curtains. He didn't wake. So, then I went in for a kiss, he slapped me away because he thought I was one of the guys messing around with him. It woke him up, as it totally startled him. It was pretty funny.

We found his room key and pulled his luggage from the underbelly of the bus. I unveiled my trip and where I had stayed, and ate, the night before. He was happy to see me and we were able to spend the entire day together in Greensboro, North Carolina. It is a beautiful place. We walked around the town and the weather was perfect.

We saw monuments and read informational bronze plaques around town about history of North Carolina. Downtown is darling. We found a local brewery next door to a massage parlor. We partook in both, and then retired to a great evening in our hotel room.

The next day I had to fly home, so we said our goodbyes a handful of times at my rental car. As I proceeded to leave, he jumped on the hood of the car, smashing his lips against the glass. It would be three more weeks before I saw him again in Florida.

*Chapter 20*

# MARCH 2011

    Kid Rock was set to play the UFC Arena on the University of Central Florida campus in Orlando, Florida. Tour had a few stops around the State, so Vince got permission for me to travel on the bus with the guys. It would be my first time traveling in the bunks. Imagine squeezing two adults into a one-man bunk! Needless to say, it was a tight fit. After a few days, I was sure that I could never live on a bus.

    The best part of the show was being able to see Jamey Johnson, perform live, with my own eyes, 'In Color". I had told Vince about Jamey Johnson when he hit the road months before, and I was right, Vince became a fan. Jamey Johnson was rough, tough, burly and unruly.

    One evening there was a hotel room brawl between Kid Rock and Jamey Johnson. Apparently, the artists managers had to pay the hotel to clean up broken furniture, wall art, and blood.

    After the show, I headed to the bus for food. There are not many places open for after-show food around one in the morning, so typically it consisted of pizza, burgers or tacos from a fast food joint. This night, was Taco Bell. I guess the guys had their fair share, because I arrived to them playing 'baseball' with hard-shelled tacos. It was funny for only a brief moment. Then my feelings switched from comedic, to feeling sorry for the University grounds keepers. Imagine coming in the next day to shredded lettuce, saucy ground beef, grated cheese and hard tortillas pieces scattered amuck. I did not want to be part of their shenanigans.

    The next day we woke up in the parking lot of the Fort Lauderdale Seminole Hard Rock. I have few memories of this place, maybe because I was too tired from lack of sleep in a small bunk, who knows. I do, however, have a memory of my new dress, my new heels and the awesome hotel pools. My new dress stands out in my memory because I noticed all the turning heads as I walked by (that doesn't happen to me *often*, as you may recall, I don't wear dresses much). I felt pretty. Secondly, I recall my heels because when I wear them I am taller than Vince. It bothers me more than it does him.

    Vince had a day off, which meant we earned the right to lounge all day with each other: no rehearsals. Later that night, when the humidity subsided, we made our way to the pools and bars. I guess we waited too long to get to the pools, because once we arrived, they were closed for the night.

    And this is the reason I remember the pools. They were so awesome! It was like paradise with amazing landscape and design. Sidewalks meandered around the pools with colorful underwater lights. There were rock formation water slides, tropical trees and greenery lining the walkways. It was dark out, but you could still see some of the landscape glowing off the pools from the underwater lights. We grabbed some drinks. I want to say I ordered something tropical with fruit and an umbrella, or maybe a fancy wine, but most likely I ordered beer, or whiskey on the rocks.

  A few drinks in, we got a wild hair and decided to help ourselves to the closed pool area. We had to be quiet, so we didn't attract the security guards. We snuck off like teenagers into the pools. We played and splashed, kissed and giggled, and swam underwater through the closed areas like peaceful mer-people.

  Vince pointed out a running water slide behind the bar that they kept on for the ambiance. The stairs to the top were too exposed to the bar, so we conjured up the idea to rock climb up the sides of the rock tower and slide down without being noticed. Vince had rock climbing experience, but I couldn't make it. Instead, I did my best climb up the slide from the bottom of the pool. I only made it half-way. Trying not to laugh at my inability to climb higher, I slid back into the water.

  I waited in the pool for Vince to come sliding down. But, just then, I notice a family on an evening walk around the pools, so I scooted to the side into a shadowed area. I wanted to shout for Vince, but I couldn't give away my hiding place. I just hope he saw the family too, as I had. Moments later I saw something swish down the water slide and float into the pool. It was his swim trunks! 'Oh shoot', I said in a quiet voice.

Then, as bare as a newborn baby, Vince rounded the corner of the slide naked! I clasped my hands over my mouth to conceal my laugh and shock. He made his debut into the pool. The family looked back when they heard the splash. But luckily, Vince was underwater swimming toward me, and they just shrugged it off as if they were mistaken by the sound, and continued walking away.

    Vince emerged and I did the universal silence motion with my finger to my lips while I giggled and pointing to the family walking away. We swam into the shadows and kissed some more before searching for his swim trunks.

*Chapter 21*

# APRIL 2011

    I am not sure if New Orleans always stinks like horse manure and vomit, or if I happened to be lucky enough to experience it on this rare occasion. Vince and I were three months into our marriage and he was now officially on the Kid Rock tour. We had originally thought this tour may be a temporary gig, and he would rejoin Jimmy Buffet after the Europe tour. But, as it turned out, Kid Rock was his new home-away-from-home.
    It was time for the annual Kid Rock Cruise and roadies were allowed to invite one guest to attend the cruise with them. I had never cruised before, so I figured I would join. All I needed was a passport, and a round trip ticket to New Orleans where the ship would berth, embarking from Port Nola.
    The ship was headed out of the country for the small Island of Cozumel, Mexico. My identification still said Bethany Jobe. In a little way I was taking David with me, as it felt, wherever I went. This wasn't an issue, in itself, as TSA just needed to see that my cruise ticket matched my identification. The real issue was only metaphysical.

I arrived in New Orleans the evening before the cruise, Vince had a hotel near Port Nola. The crew had all their gear in, what I called, the underbelly of the ship. Gear was loaded separately from the passenger luggage, absolved of customs inspection. The crew hid liquor and other recreational substances, which would not pass through inspection, into gear cases, and then loaded them onto the ship.

Little rumor: back in the mid-seventies when touring acts started with Sound Image, they would smuggle drugs in gear cases to make extra cash. Sound Image was one of the first touring sound companies to be debt free because of their side hustle. They survived the eighties market crash because they didn't have business loans like other touring sound companies. The rock-n-roll world is a crazy place.

After the crew was done loading gear, we hit the French Quarter for some dinner. Along the roadside was piled horse manure from the mounted police patrols. Added to the manure smell, was the smell of vomit, from late night party-goers. I can tell you that the smell was so offensive I lost my appetite. It was sheer luck finding a half-way decent restaurant away from the repulsive smells of the alleyways and streets.

A fellow sound engineer, Beau, came out with us to find dinner. He's a handsome, big rugged guy. I was strangely attracted to his quietly cavalier demeanor. He hardly ever said a thing, and when he did, I was never sure if he was serious. He wore jeans, a simple tee-shirt, and a ballcap. He once wore shorts and I saw his Marvin-the-Martian tattoo on his leg. I chuckled as it seemed like a tattoo you would only get if you were drunk (and I'm a professional on bad tattoo choices). Beau was also tall, a protector-ish type, so I felt safe walking with him and Vince amid the rotten smell of the streets.

After dinner we walked looking for a bar, as I recall, it was a bar Beau had been meaning to find, not one we found by accident (although it felt like an accident). We walked off Bourbon Street down a thin dark side-street, which actually may have been an alley. The entry was dark and creaky, like walking into Halloween, but it wasn't October. It was called the Dungeon. I didn't like it. We ordered drinks just inside the door at a downstairs bar, and didn't venture much further.

While the guys waited for their drinks, I turned around from the bar, with my drink, to see a guy walk in who could have been Nicholas Cage. He smiled at me and nodded with a "helllloo" smile as he walked by, two guys trailing behind him. I put on my thinking face, and decided it was Nicholas Cage.

I swung around and said to Beau and Vince,

"I just saw Nicholas Cage, and I think he flirted with me!".

It was a bit of an over exaggeration because his smile and nod felt flirtatious but I'm sure it was just a friendly hello. The guys didn't believe me and by the time they turned around, we only saw the backs of the guys following him, turn the corner. I said I wasn't joking and we should follow them so I could prove it. They had gone to the upstairs bar. The bartender overhead me, and confirmed it was indeed Nicholas Cage.

"He frequents here." The bartended settled it.

"I knew it! I think he flirted with me?" By now, just joking to get a reaction.

We all three decided we should take our drinks upstairs to explore and the guys could confirm it was indeed Nick. Since I was on was first name basis with Nick, I shortened his name jokingly. Then I dropped his name as we headed upstairs several times, pretending that Nick and I were long-time friends.

"Nick comes here all the time guys. I've seen Nick here before. I wonder why Nick comes here, this place is kind of gross."

My joking became irritating, but funny at the same time.

We walked up a dark staircase, which was slightly uneven, leaning to the left, approached the upper bar, and we saw Nick and his two pals, or body guards (it would be hard to tell which, for certain). There were only a handful of other people in the tiny upper bar. We looked around, as if sincerely checking out the place, and headed back downstairs.

Again, I voiced my disdain for the venue, we finished our drinks and headed back to the hotel.

I know that Kid Rock was also walking around The French Quarter with his 'pals' (body guards). It's hard to tell who your real friends are when you rise to fame (especially if you didn't have real ones to start with). It's something I've noticed with famous people;

accountability gets lost when 'yes-men' follow them around trying to kiss their butt. Then, with no accountability, they act-out and become crazy. Sometimes their craziness is even reinforced by the silence, or encouragement, of the 'yes-men' around them. This is my professional opinion (and I am becoming quite the professional).

The following week I googled Nick to see if he lived near the French Quarter in New Orleans. Apparently, he does have a house there, and that very evening, after we saw him, he was arrested. The news said: 'Domestic abuse, disturbing the peace and public drunkenness.' According to police, 'Cage was heavily intoxicated and violent, arguing with his wife, Alice Kim, in a tattoo parlor and on the street. Later, he punched a few cars.' I guess I missed adding another memory to my tattoo collection that night with Nick.

# The Roadie Wife

*Chapter 22*

# CRUISIN' ALONG

The next day was an early rise. The normal passengers had to go through TSA, while the crew were setting up for the Kid Rock Bon Voyage show. I stood in a long line of excited Kid Rock fans. As each fan passed through TSA and made their way onto the ship, they stopped for a customary commemorative photo with Kid Rock. It was his way saying, 'We are stuck on this cruise together for five days.' 'Look at me.' 'Touch me.' 'And then leave me alone.' Albeit, he never said those words. I pushed around the photo line to avoid the awkward exchange, and went to find my cabin.

After getting settled, I found my credentials and went off to the main deck where Vince and Beau were done setting up the stage and had begun testing the gear. Departure was soon and the five-day party would commence down the Mississippi into Mexico, and back.

I felt seasick and we hadn't even set sail yet. I was told by everyone I mentioned it to, that it was just my imagination. The only person who believed me was a literal Rocket Scientist, who was the wife of another sound engineer. She worked at NASA and told me there would be some residual movement that could cause sea sickness for sensitive people (I guess I was sensitive).

"Despite the massive size of this cruise line, movement can still be felt." She said.

Back in her cabin she had a pill that NASA's gives astronauts when they practice in the anti-gravity chamber. She assured me that I could find her later if I needed one to help with the dizzy feeling.

Over the course of the next few days, I saw things that cannot be unseen. Of course, I didn't mind listening to Gretchen Wilson, or sitting across from her during breakfast in private catering. I enjoyed hearing the hilarious Carlos Mencia, who had been underground since his plagiarism accusations. I loved the unlimited twenty-four-hour soft serve ice cream and exotic buffet food. Vince worked almost the entire cruise, so I ended up being alone a lot. I took naps, read a book and really tried to enjoy myself.

At the gym, the treadmill faced the rounded windows out the front of the boat. For any average person, this would be spectacular feeling, like you're running into the ocean. However, it made me more seasick. When I left the gym, I saw sign-ups for a lap dancing class that was being held by some famous dancer. This class is not offered on a normal Carnival cruise, but this whole cruise was anything but normal. I shrugged, 'what the heck' and signed up.

Later, I grabbed my required high-heels and joined twenty other ladies, each sitting in a chair waiting for the instructor. Almost everyone wore their heels and yoga pants to class. I wore flip-flops and carried my heels. We got ready and the teacher began to show us some simple moves to an erotic song.

It was hard not to laugh, mostly at ourselves, but we ended up having a good time and it was actually moderately aerobic. Heck, even if I hadn't planned on using the techniques at some point, at least I got a good workout.

I decided I would *try* my new lap dance skills later that night when Vince had a break. His time off was awkwardly in the middle of the evening, after dinner, before the night gig, before bedtime.

I asked him to sit in the middle of our small cabin in the desk chair and I put on some music (the sexiest song I had was a country song downloaded on my phone). I had on my little lingerie, high heels and did my best not to laugh as I put my lesson into practice; kissing his neck, and doing my newly acquired fancy footwork.

Then, in my heels, I lost my balance and fell flat on my butt. I looked up from the floor, and we both burst into laughter. It was just what we needed.

My courage must have been a turn-on, because it aroused a good laugh and a romantic romp. Vince had to return to work, but we stretched out every minute and cherished what time we had together.

Sometime the next day when Vince was on break, we went for a quick drink by the pool. On our way, we saw my dance instructor. I told her what had happened with 'my moves' and she laughed.
Then in all seriousness she asked,
"But did you get the desired end result?".
I laughed and confirmed I had.
"That's all that matters honey!" She smiled.

*Chapter* 23

# SUN AND MOON

It wasn't until day three that I found my NASA lady, for the anti-woozy medicine, before docking in Cozumel. Thank goodness for her pill...and for a non-moving surface.

It was a beautiful day, and luckily, Vince had two hours off before setting up for the island show. We made a sprint for the shore, found some guys renting scooters, and snagged two before anyone else had a chance. I was so happy to be on land.

We took-off out of sight, down the coastline, and followed a little rickety wooden arrow pointing off the main road toward the sand carved: 'Drinks & Food'. We emerged from the palm trees, and tropical shrubbery, to behold blue translucent water. I could see the tropical fish swimming at sea. It was breathtaking

The blue ocean was such a contrast against the booming white sand. It was just perfect. We splashed around in the water, just enough to cool off from the heat, had some drinks and tacos, and laid out in the sun for a while. I could have stayed there all day!

It wasn't long before we had to head back. I was on my scooter, alive and in love. A gorgeous day with my new husband cruising down an amazing tropical Mexican island. Back at the pier, he headed off to work, so I headed back to the cabin for some rest.

Over the course of the cruise, Vince and I had met a sweet couple from Sydney. The couple worked for the cruise line, and were *also* newly married. They invited us to tour their living quarters after the island show. Vince and I planned to meet them once Vince was back on the ship at their designated employee entrance.

The sun was setting and all the passengers were returning to the ship. The evening was booming: music, bar games, gambling, drinking, standup comedy, and night swimming. At fifteen stories tall, the ship was like a city!

I was able to navigate my way, to meet Vince, through the crowds chanting the Kid Rock Cruise mantra, 'I'm on a boat mother-*#@*er'! ... and blocked my eyes as I passed anything seedy or risqué. Good rule of thumb: just ignore anything that looked questionable, or odd, when walking around the ship.

I found Vince and we headed to see the Australians for *our* behind-the-scenes tour. The couple had a tiny cabin room, and shared small living quarters, not unlike roadies. But, it felt like a submarine, because they had no windows. The underbelly was packed with off-duty cruise employees bustling around, living normal life: playing games, reading, lounging, eating dinner.

The Australians told us this Kid Rock Cruise had spent a record amount of money on alcohol; higher than any other cruise before. I was shocked, but it wasn't hard to believe.

Talking with these two precious Australians, caused me to reflect on my newly married times with David in Australia. How David was always wanting to go, and see, and do, but never wanting to settle down. I wondered again if I could have made it work with him somehow, if I had been more creative.

When Vince and I completed our tour in the staff quarters, we headed out to have some quiet time. The only place we could find was the top deck of the ship. It was a smaller section of the boat, open aired and more secluded - darkened and shut down. Since all the activities were on the lower decks by this time, there was no one in sight.

We found the miniature golf course and putted for a bit, then found an unmanned bar with a small blue kiddie wading pool full of melting ice, and blue Bud Lite bottles. We snagged some beer (even though we never drank Bud Lite), and walked around with our blue bottles telling stories about the ungodly things we had seen throughout the day.

"I think I saw a couple having sex during the concert in the middle of the crowd!" I exclaimed.

We both laughed knowing I hadn't been mistaken. Then, we started making out in a dark area and thought, if those people could do it in a crowd, we could do it up there. I honestly would *never* have sex in a crowd of people, on a secluded beach, yes. On the top of an empty ship – maybe. But, not in a crowd. Then, one-thing-led-to-the-next, and in a shadowed area on top of the ship... the moonlight and night sky were our only witnesses.

*Chapter 24*

# SUMMERTIME

    I flew home after the cruise to a busy spring full of my philanthropy efforts. I was planning my third annual human anti-trafficking event, going through master life coaching, training to be a volunteer court appointed service advocate, and attending a meet-up for second wives of husbands with kids. Vince arrived back in New Orleans to continue the Kid Rock tour. I didn't see him again until he flew home for a tour break in early May. Then he headed out again on a three-week Canadian tour.

    I look back now and know why I was keeping myself so busy. There was a theme to fill my time – each pointed to a greater need within me. I had not known, at the time, I was telling a story through my 'doing', instead of through my 'being'.

    Vince got word that he would be working the 2011 Country Music Awards. I had watched the CMT's since I was a kid and had a love for country music. I was so jealous. I used to swear David would end up playing a music award show, and that would be my way of attending an event like that. Obviously, even if David ended up going to one, I wouldn't be the person he invited now. This was my chance as a roadie wife, but I wasn't invited. It had me wishing for a roadie skill so *I* could attend the show.

Kid Rock was scheduled to perform his new duo with Cheryl Crow, "Collide". It wasn't as good as their first duo, "Picture", but not too shabby. I wasn't a fan of many Kid Rock songs, but I would listen to "Picture" during my break-up with David, and cry, and hit replay – that song and, Avril Lavigne, "Happy Ending", were two top songs on my sorrow sound track (yes, I had one of those). I can barely listen to either of those songs anymore. Needless to say, the CMT Award show was just another work day for Vince and the crew... and just another work day for me back home.

Vince's daughters arrived mid-June for their summer visitation with their dad. Since he would only be around for part of the visit, I would have them linger with me for some summer family activities. If it wasn't for the taxing custody issues with his ex-wife, I would have been feeling accomplished and satisfied with the life we were making. As it was, I was doing my best in the step-mother category.

Though the summer was filled, it wasn't too long before I started browsing the tour schedule again. It felt like I hadn't seen Vince since the cruise because our days were so full, even when he was home. So, after I delivered the girls to their mother, I planned to hop a flight to Omaha, Nebraska mid-July. Vince would have a few days off and we could catch up in a hotel, instead of in his bunk, on route to another destination.

I happened to arrive in Omaha during a heat wave. It was my first time there and I really wanted to see the town. We stayed in a downtown hotel, so we were able to walk to most places. The town was gorgeous. I've often thought about moving there since my visit. We were those crazy tourists, as it was mentioned to us at nearly every place we went.

"Why in the world are you walking around in this heat?!" Locals asked.

All the restaurants closed their patio seating due to the extreme heat, but we were silly enough to keep walking around, sweating.

We found an 'open house', and since I am a real estate broker, my boss told me to gather some real estate information and he could use my trip as a business expense. The place was a hundred- year-old industrial building in the middle of downtown that had been renovated into condos.

They had high ceilings, brick interior walls, barn doors, open concept and gorgeous views of the town. It was also a nice break from the heat... and they provided refreshments. We looked at four models, collected brochures, and then re-entered the heat wave. I would dream of living in Omaha for months after my trip was over.

Come to think of it, maybe I should look into moving to Omaha again.

The Roadie Wife

*Chapter* 25

# BEHIND THE SCENES

    Victoria and I were actually together the day we met Vince and Andrew. Sound Image was donating audio gear, and two engineers, for the bands at our event, Justice Day. Victoria and I were busy running around setting up for our first annual Justice Day, when two audio engineers, who were assigned to help us, appeared backstage. I sped walked to tell Victoria.
    "Two good lookin' audio guys just arrived backstage. You *need* to go check-em' out." I jeered.
    I told her I would have dated either one of them, upon first look, but Vince was the only one who asked.
    Even though I started dating Vince, Andrew had stayed friends with Victoria and I after the event.
    Andrew happened to be filling-in as a substitute technician, with Vince, on the Kid Rock tour. The last week of July, Vince and Andrew would have a tour stop in Irvine. After Irvine, the tour would have a few days off before their next show in San Diego. This meant a hotel in downtown San Diego!

Although Andrew wanted to take his days off and go home to rest in his own bed, Vince and I wanted to take *his* days off in the hotel downtown. The tour bus was headed to the hotel in San Diego after Irvine, so Andrew asked Victoria to bring-up his car to the Irvine show.

Victoria agreed to bring Andrews car to Irvine, and then meet up for dinner in crew catering (Victoria's favorite part of gigs) with the guys. After dinner, Victoria found her way to the VIP area at side stage and proceeded to get into some 'Victoria-shenanigans', rubbing elbows, and chatting with Lance Armstrong and David Spade. Lance Armstrong had been dating Cheryl Crow, who was on tour with Kid Rock, so Lance would attend several shows during that season.

Little fun fact about David Spade: he and Kid Rock were in the movie, "Joe Dirt" together. "Joe Dirt" happened to be a favorite of David and mine and we would quote lines from that movie incessantly! I wanted to go up to him and say a line from the movie, but I didn't want to be awkward (here again, the story would have been better if I had).

The next day, Vince and I made our way to the San Diego Gaslamp District to our tour-paid, boutique hotel, The Palomar. Kid Rock was set to play San Diego before they journeyed over to Arizona, and then tour steadily through mid-September. So, we spent our time pretending we were not from San Diego and immensely enjoyed ourselves.

Our friends, Wendy and Jeff, lived only a hop from the stadium where Kid Rock was set to play, so we invited them out to join us. Victoria agreed to skip this show, and babysit for Wendy and Jeff. It was a warm August evening and we were all having a great time hanging out back stage, showing them inside the tour bus, and eating dinner in crew catering.

There is a part of the Kid Rock concert that is not so family friendly. In each town, for each show, a designated roadie would go into the town and recruit dancers to 'perform' on stripper poles behind the band for one of Kid Rocks' songs. Every show has different dancers, most of them are rated PG, and they were *more-or-less* just dancing.

I am not sure where the roadie found these particular dancers, but they may have been the 'main attraction' over the song that evening. I looked at Wendy and Jeff with my jaw hanging, and eyes widened, admittedly embarrassed during this part of the show. I had to look away on several occasions. Vince recalled the crew standing backstage, wide-eyed, stuck in a trance, with their upward gaze toward the poles. I shivered to think about who cleaned those poles afterwards, summer sweat and all.

# The Roadie Wife

# Chapter 26

# AUGUST 2011

Have you ever been stuck in an elevator? I don't mean stuck, like it stopped working. But stuck, in the way that you feel captive. I've heard people describe the feeling before, but never experienced it firsthand until I was in Detroit, Michigan. Victoria and I had flown out to Detroit to meet Vince on tour. The plan was to meet-up at their big show at Tigers Stadium, and then ride along on the tour bus to Blossom Hill, Ohio for their next show at the Blossom Hill Amphitheatre. It would be Victoria's first time traveling on the tour bus with us, and we were both excited for the journey.

Victoria and I flew all day and arrived in Detroit around dinnertime. We made our way to the hotel through unknown territory, and Vince was at the venue (we wouldn't expect him back until the wee hours of the morning).

We browsed the room service menu and picked juicy hamburgers, crisp fries and a bottle of wine. We drank and ate to our hearts content. Before we readied ourselves for bed, we had a good jump on the mattress like little kids. We tired ourselves out, and called it quits. Vince had kindly ordered a roll-out bed for Victoria, which was made-up and ready for sleeping.

I don't remember falling asleep, so I know I was tired. I was so zonked out, that I didn't even notice when Vince got back from the venue. I woke as silver sunlight peeked through the opening at the curtain edge and rolled over to see Vince's sleeping head on the pillow facing me. I looked up to see Victoria had already slipped out of the room to find the complimentary breakfast in the lobby. Oh, how she loves food! Especially free food. She also knew I hadn't seen my husband in weeks, so she would take her time at breakfast, on purpose for me. At this, I took the chance to wake my love, to make love.

As we lay there comfortably in each other's arms, he lightened the mood.

"I thought Victoria was dead when I came into the room last night and saw her on the cot!" He said.

"Why?" I laughed.

"She was lying flat on her back with her arms crossed over her chest like a mummy. I thought she was either dead, or maybe she was a vampire about to pop up and flash her teeth at me."

I bellowed with laughter.

We showered and made our way to the lobby, newlyweds in love.

We saw the crew in the lobby still sitting with Victoria, so we joined them. Jokes and banter went on until the bus arrived: like a school bell, the tables cleared and the guys headed out to pile into their bus. Victoria and I would follow the bus in our rental car.

Victoria navigated the parking lot around the back of the loading dock. She parked, and we made our way through backstage security, to where the crew was getting ready for sound check. I am not a sports fan, but I could imagine someone who loved the Detroit Tigers would have loved cruising around every corner of that stadium.

There are corporate box seats and rooms along the top of the stadium, like many stadiums, with an elevator that opened right into the room. This is where they had band and crew catering. Victoria headed up to catering before me (of course). The weather started looking very stormy. But, I hung with Vince until the crew began scrambling across the stage. I figured I had better move out of the way and go join Victoria for lunch. I wasn't familiar with Midwest weather, and how often it changes, sometimes momentarily. But, the audio crew began covering gear with plastic sheeting, so they must have been aware a summer storm would hit any moment. I crossed the field behind the security fences and made my way to the private elevator that went up to catering.

Stepping into the elevator alone, I pressed the button for corporate boxes and the door began to shut. I was humming while wondering what I would eat. Then, a hand grabbed the door and hollered, 'Hold up!' pushing the doors back open. It was Gio. I knew him. I liked him. We would chill when he wasn't on Kid Rock detail. But, he was on detail and Kid Rock entered the elevator behind him. We exchanged friendly nods, and the doors began to shut.

Elevators are awkward enough, without being stuck in one, to stare at the ceiling, trying not to make eye contact, picking at the paint, for a brief sixty-second ride, *with* your husbands' boss. I wanted to stay a wallflower. I didn't want him to ask me whose wife I was, or be noticed in any way.

But, what I did next, may have made me more conspicuous than I preferred. This time as the doors were shutting, I grabbed the doors and pushed them open… and just walked away. Walked away, just like it was my plan the whole time. I chuckled, imagining them both shrugging to each other, and then nonchalantly checking if they had armpit odor, or bad breath. I waited a few minutes for the elevator to come back down, then went up alone. Gio and I exchanged knowing smirks up in catering. I just laughed and went to find Victoria.

Victoria would be upset if I don't include the next part. It did begin to storm, and early-arriving fans were murmuring down on the field, everyone thought the show would be cancelled. And, that's not good if you're from Detroit, performing in Detroit: Kid Rock was both. Victoria could be seen 'discretely' praying, hands outstretched toward the storm, for it all to cease. I knew enough about my best friend, to just let her do her thing.

Lo and behold, within fifteen minutes the storm subsided, clouds passed and blue skies appeared. Crew took down the plastic and the sunshine dried up the field. The show would go on. Okay… maybe that's how Midwest storms come and go?! Or maybe it was Victoria's prayer… miraculous things happen all the time.

*Chapter 27*

# HIGH ROLLIN

By the next day, Victoria had made friends with the security guards, crew, and some band members in Detroit. She would be bunking in the 'junk bunk' to Ohio. A 'junk bunk' is an empty bunk, where crew throw all their 'junk' that they don't want laying around the bus.

The guys were nice enough to move their junk for her to crash with us on the bus into Blossom Hill, Ohio. We stayed up late drinking through the night, riding one of six, Kid Rock tour buses, in caravan to Ohio.

The next morning, okay... mid-day, I woke up and Victoria was already gone from the bus. She was nowhere to be found. I thought for sure she'd be down in catering. When I found Vince, it became apparent he hadn't seen her either. So, I started asking around until I heard one of the guys say they saw her go with a runner somewhere. She didn't take her phone, so I was left to wait and wonder.

In the meantime, I explored the Blossom Hill Amphitheatre. It is beautiful, and if you've never been, I highly recommend it. It's an extraordinary half dome, made of wood. I was enjoying myself, walking around the venue with a cool drink, taking in the summer humidity with all the sights and smells.

A few hours later a blacked-out Escalade pulled into the back-parking lot, and Victoria jumped out of the passenger-side.

"Where have you been?" I hollered to her.
"We had to run errands." She yelled back.
She was so nonchalant and matter-of-fact.
"Who? Who had to run errands?" I questioned.
But, she just walked toward me in her cool sunglasses, holding her Frappuccino. She was swaying her hips as she turned back, mid-sip, to wave goodbye to the runner. She's a stranger to no-one and no-place.

I guess it was a good thing she met the runner, because later we hitched a ride to our car rental location in town. Unfortunately, they didn't have the standard sedan I had reserved. So, Victoria and I *had* to drive a new Mercedes (oh bummer) back to the airport. We played, 'rock-paper-scissors' to see who would drive: she won. It didn't matter though, I was high-rolling, as her passenger, to the Cleveland Airport.

*Chapter 28*

# MOONSHINE

    I flew into Houston for a show in Woodlands, Texas the first week of September. I would be traveling on the tour bus from Woodlands to Orange Beach, Alabama. Then I would fly home after the Orange Beach show. It was a long weekend for Labor Day and I had an extra day off. I figured even though Kid Rock wasn't staying in one city long, Vince could squeeze me into his bunk and we could spend a few days together (I guess this would be our conscious coupling).
    The Woodlands was Wanda's hometown. Robert contacted Vince to get Wanda and her friend's tickets to see Kid Rock. In addition, Vince thought it would be sweet to get them all backstage passes.
    However, by the time they arrived, I had already sampled my share of homemade moonshine from mason jars on the bus, and I was on my way to not remembering much. There was plum moonshine. Peach moonshine. And… well, more moonshine. It was hard to drink because it burned significantly on the way down my throat. But, I still managed to sample them all, for moonshine sake, of course.

I think subconsciously, I just didn't want to see Wanda and her friends – or maybe better put – not be present to see Wanda and her friends.

Later, I decided to make my way to side-stage and embarked on a blurry journey along the tall bushes that lined the dimly lit dirt path, from the tour bus to the venue. Before I reached the security guards, I began to feel a little creeped-out in the darkness of the surrounding bushes (my moonshine was getting the best of me). Suddenly, I saw two black snakes down on the path and I went running for my life. The only thing that stopped me mid-sprint was the laughing security guards. That's when I realized it was a practical joke. I punched one in the arm on my way, in my fidgety drunk, anger humor.

Sadly, on my way back to the bus, I forgot about the damn practical joke, and the same scare caused me to jump back in fright, yet again.

Maybe it was my anger at those damn rubber snakes (or the prankster security guards), but I decided to pick a fight with Vince. I suppose seeing Wanda made me think of Robert in Irvine, enough to ask Vince about his ex-fling, as we boarded the bus. It started a short back-and-forth spat about him being gone all the time and me being ignorant at home. He retorted that I could be having a fling at home, just as easily, as him having one on the road. Touché. Irritated, I switched the subject to the news on the bus TV.

Warnings were coming over the airwaves that Orange Beach was on red alert for the Tropical Storm Lee. We began hearing chatter that the show in Orange Beach would be canceled, the buses would go straight onto Green Bay, Wisconsin. This created a travel snafu, because my flight would be departing from Pensacola in two days. It was too late to do anything about my flight, so I made a mental note to deal with it the next morning: call my boss to let him know my trip was headed North.

After the show, we loaded into the bus and inhaled some after-show food. The buses and trucks were loaded and being readied for the two-day trip up the United States. Once we were all exhausted and drunk, we climbed into bunks. Vince and I had to spoon in order to fall asleep without falling out of the bunk. It was a little unnerving trying not to roll out, it would have been a far fall from the third bunk. I decided, if I *did* fall, I would just stay on the floor, because getting back up would have proved an impossible task, sober it was tough, drunk – not happening. I kept thinking, 'moonshine was a bad choice'.

The Roadie Wife

# Chapter 29

# TABLE DANCING

    I ended up on the top of the bar, dancing, at Coyote Ugly because of a tour detour (I feel like I could make a joke about this - tour detour - what do you call coming off tour? A de-tour. No? Not funny?).

    The next afternoon we were awakened by other crew members. We were in Memphis, Tennessee, at a hotel downtown and we had to leave the bus. Now that the Orange Beach show had been cancelled, the crew had an extra day off and the tour manager reserved rooms for everyone at the Westin. I was excited because this was a surprise, and I had never been to Memphis before. The bus underbelly doors were open, we departed, grabbed our luggage from the compartment, and headed inside to get our room key from the tour manager. After showering, we set out to find food. In the lobby we met up with other crew thinking the same thing: lunch. So, a group of us hit the streets together.

    Memphis is notorious for jazz roots, amazing po'boys, and fried crawfish. The area is filled with soul and you can feel it as you walk the streets, between brick buildings, storefronts and restaurants. We located a redbrick corner restaurant. The walls were covered with jazz paraphernalia, and it had a huge outdoor bar patio with dueling pianos.

Tucking into a corner table, we inspected the menu and decided on oysters for appetizers - oysters soaked in pepper vodka! We were not disappointed. The vodka slightly cooks the oyster like lemon juice on seafood, it was like taking a shot of seasoned ocean-goodness. Yes, Memphis is landlocked (which is what I was thinking). So, where do they get their oysters? Well, let me tell you what I found out: the Mississippi River runs along Memphis, follow that down to where the River enters the Gulf of Mexico... and this is where Memphis Oysters come from. I've never had oysters so good, or big... and that's my professional opinion.

Vince and I spent the remainder of the day carousing from place-to-place, meeting up with other crew, and band members, along the way. By evening we were looking for food again and ended up at Coyote Ugly with two other audio engineers. At some point we finished our food and moved over to the bar to have a drink before calling it a night.

Then it happened! Some song came on. I had never been to a Coyote Ugly, so I glanced around to see what was meant to happen next. The bartender told the song indicated it was time for the ladies in the house to get up on the bar and do a little dance... and I was the *only* lady in the house (it was a slow weekday evening). I hadn't even known there was *a* song. I looked around, when it struck me, people (guys) were cheering in *my* direction.

Not just *any* cheer, a cheer-encouragement to climb up on the bar. I started shaking my head: no, not me, you're all terribly mistaken! I am not climbing up on that bar.

The more I resisted, in pure terror by the way, the more it encouraged the crowd. I felt like Cameron Diaz in the movie, "My Best Friend's Wedding", when they were at the bar and wanted her to sing Karaoke. Except, I wasn't Cameron Diaz, and I didn't dance or sing. I had to do something to stop the raging crowd. I would either have to run-out of the place, or get up on the bar.

Taking in a deep breath, I reluctantly climbed up on my swiveling bar stool (Vince kindly held my chair, so I didn't fall before I performed) and swung-up onto the bar top. I remember closing my eyes and doing something like the funky-chicken for a *brief* few wiggles. The crowd roared and clapped and cheered, for what felt like a century, before I reached out for help off the bar, all-the-while shaking my head in disapproval, turning red, and smiling in pure shame.

The next day we embarked on our journey toward Green Bay, Wisconsin. I had already found a flight from Green Bay, and let my boss know I would be away for a few more days. Orange Beach was lucky, but I was not. Due to the fact the storm never made landfall, the airlines made me pay full price for a new ticket.

Buses drove into Green Bay before dinner the next day, and to my surprise, the tour manager reserved Vince and I a really nice room with a jacuzzi tub. I was a high-roller again! We enjoyed the lasting moments we had together, because they would slip away too quickly.

Since Vince had to work a show the next day, it left me to navigate my way to the airport without him. I landed in San Diego, drove home to my empty condo, and went to bed. The next day I woke up to a power outage. I went into the office to see if power was on there. It wasn't. We waited awhile to see if it would resume. After a few hours, we tuned into the radio to hear power was out from San Diego, all the way to Orange county, and parts of Arizona. We closed-up shop for the day and it left me wishing I had stayed in Wisconsin.

I went home and did some reading to pass the time, waiting for power to turn on. It didn't. I began to wonder how I would cook dinner in an all-electric condo. I remembered that Vince had a camping BBQ somewhere. I found it, and grilled myself a steak with asparagus.

It started to get dark when Victoria called to check on me. Her parents had a generator and invited me over to huddle up in case riots broke out in town (which seemed to be an over exaggeration).

Sometimes I didn't mind sulking alone. But, today, I chose card games and wine with Victoria, her parents and a handful of their neighbors. We stayed up well past an average weeknight – and talked about end-of-world chaos. Conspiracy loves company.

It would later be called the Southwest Blackout; it was eleven hours long, and the largest blackout in California history to date.

*Chapter 30*

# OCTOBER 2011

Vince and I had decided when we eloped, that we would wait a year to go on a honeymoon since life was busy during our eloping season. Life was essentially busy all the time, but we needed to make time for ourselves that wasn't on a bus or tour stop.

I found a cute vacation rental in Todos Santos, Mexico. It was an above-garage-apartment in a gated home owners community called, Rancho Nuevo, along a five-mile private beach. The beach stretched the length of the Mexico peninsula in the small coastal town up from Cabo San Lucas in the foothills of the Sierra de la Laguna Mountains. It was simple, sparsely populated, and just what we were looking for. The directions they sent were as follows:

*Some cautions for driving in this area: Watch for free-range cattle and goats that wander across the highway. Outside the city, a left-turn signal often means it is safe to pass the vehicle giving the signal. So, if you want to turn left, as into Rancho Nuevo, if there is traffic behind you it is best to exit to the right, across from the Rancho Nuevo entrance, wait for the traffic to pass and cross over the highway to enter.*

What seemed like out-of-nowhere, we spotted the short stucco walls with Rancho Nuevo written on either side. It had entry gates in the open position. We laughed because there were gates, but no fences in either direction. Vince pulled off the poorly maintained highway, onto the dirt road, and followed the address indicators around to the ocean and parked in the gravel driveway of a Spanish-styled custom home.

The hosts, Gunther and Melanie, greeted us upon arrival, informing us they live full-time in the main house if we needed anything. Melanie said, once we were settled to join them for evening drinks under their pool side palapa. Melanie and Gunther were in their sixties. He was from Germany and she was from Seattle, Washington. They had built their home along the beach as a secluded get away from fast pace life. It was just that. The site was beautiful and we could hear, and see, crashing waves from our second story patio, and from inside our rental through the expansive windows.

Their palapa was so big it covered their outdoor furniture and BBQ area. It was made of long palm fronds that were connected in the middle to a large tree stump with supporting beams around the outside parameter. We sipped homemade margaritas, as they told us about the private beach from cliff-to-cliff, the clothing optional rule, beach goats, whales migrating, sea turtle hatchings, the steep ocean drop-off, and strong rip-tides. We liked them right away. They were hip and unconventional.

They asked if we wanted to schedule a massage in our room for the following day and if we wanted to buy from the neighborhood fish monger when he passed through their area. Melanie told us about the small market and the local restaurant, which was more like a big homey dining room with humble owners as chefs and servers. We wanted to try it all!

Todos Santos was not a vacation destination, it was a small farming and fishing community, some distance from attractions, and not easy to travel into from La Paz or Cabo San Lucas.

We visited the local restaurant Melanie recommended and were the only guests in the entire place, which did not come as a surprise. The server presented the wine menu and we used our best Spanglish (Spanish / English), to communicate, and they did too. Upon choosing a wine, we overheard the owner send the server to the mercado for the bottle we chose. We insisted he not make special arrangements for us, but they wouldn't have it any other way. We waited for a short while until the server arrived with our selection and presented so eloquently. It was the humblest establishment I've ever had the pleasure of experiencing – we were treated as King and Queen. I fell in love with their native hospitality instantly.

Vince wanted to buy some fresh caught fish - he enjoys cooking - so we enjoyed shopping and cooking our own meals when traveling. The following day Melanie told us the monger was passing through their community. We ran down like kids meeting the ice cream man. The monger jumped into the bed of his truck, opened three ice chests full of fresh fish on ice for us to view. Vince picked out some menu items, handed him cash, and the monger closed-up and drove off.

Melanie gave us directions to the mercado in town, about a five-minute drive, across the sandy main highway along the blue ocean. In town, we found the small mercado with fresh limes, avocados, cilantro, garlic and other native fruits and vegetables. The town was humble and welcoming. Small, dark-skinned people turned their heads as we walked down the dusty streets through their small town. It was warm, and barefoot children ran across the street in front of us, eating melting ice cream.

We decided to walk around for a while. Peeking into shops, we found locally rolled cigars – we bought some. Every shop seemed to stock traditional Spanish ceramic pottery decorated with brightly colored sea turtles, sun and moon designs, and several sizes of clay pots.

We stumbled across a small taco stand with an older wrinkly lady cooking on a flat hot surface, dirt underfoot. It smelled tantalizing. She had a few bar stools along the sidewalk against a rickety old bar under a palapa. The palapa was the same design as the one at our rental house, but a fraction of the size. We stopped and peered over the bar to inspect.

"¿Qué estás cocinado?" We asked what she was making.

"Mixtos." She replied (or that's what we think she said).

There were fresh rolled tortilla dough balls nearby as she was flipping hot flat ones on her grille. Chopped white onions, fresh red tomatoes and juicy meat were in small bowls on her tabletop. The smell of garlic, lime, and chilis filled my nostrils. I can almost taste it now. We each ordered two mixtos and pulled up bars stools to watch her put together our plates with sides of Mexican rice and refried beans.

After we had our fill, we walked into the next building with a sign: "Hotel California". We both chuckled, looked at each other, and simultaneously asked "*Thee* Hotel California?"

It was beautiful and had little shops along the length of the courtyard. We peeked in all the shops, bought a few more cigars, and made our way back to the car. We decided jokingly, it must not have been *Thee* Hotel California, because we were able to leave.

# The Roadie Wife

*Chapter 31*

# DELICATE THINGS

We arrived back to Gunther and Melanie's place in time to relax before our scheduled in-home massages. Melanie greeted us and said my sister had called, leaving the message to call her back. Melanie had provided us her landline for family in case of emergency. I had a pit in my stomach when she said my sister had called because it meant there must have been an emergency. I immediately called her back. She greeted me solemnly.

"Bethany, Grandpa passed away." She said.

We both went silent for a moment.

"What happened?" I asked.

My lip quivered and my eyes swelled with tears.

Vince was looking across at me with questioning eyebrows, waiting for me to tell him what I had heard.

"He had a massive heart attack last night. The ambulance got there super quick. But he died on the way to the hospital, and they couldn't revive him. I am so sorry Bethany." She said.

My sister and I exchanged condolences and agreed to catch up when I returned home. She was sorry to call, but knew it was important for me to know. And it was. She knew how close Paisano and I had become over the years. How I never stopped seeing Paisano, even after my dad stopped speaking to him, and told us kids we would no longer see Grandpa anymore. How I used to ride my bike to visit him before I was old enough to drive. How he had come to love David, and even Josh. Paisano never met a stranger and had a wonderful Italian connection with my best friend, Victoria. He had encouraged me to date again after my divorce, welcoming Vince fondly, and gladly became Paisano, as Vince nicknamed him.

Grandpa Paisano *wasn't* always a nice man. He found Jesus later in life and was working out forgiveness and kindness. I admire someone who wants to change and make amends with those they wronged. I think my dad took offense to the change, maybe as in, "too little too late". Or maybe my dad was so saturated with sorrow because Paisano wasted so many years on women, money and rage. Maybe my dad couldn't handle the thought of offering forgiveness to Paisano late in life. Now, again, it seemed my dad was left standing holding the short straw.

Relationships are hard to understand, and I don't blame my dad for pulling away from his father. But in this moment, I couldn't help but think of the grief my dad might be feeling. He was still estranged from his own father, and it was too late to remedy.

I knew what Paisano meant to me. I had no regrets with Paisano. Tears fell, but not for myself, at this point, they were for my dad. Death makes you contemplate many things: regrets... lost time. It may seem strange, but death must be grappled with while you are still alive. After death, is too late.

My scheduled massage was perfect timing after the news about Paisano. I hung up the phone and readied myself for some decompressing. Vince and I had our massages at the same time, but we each picked different spots on the property: his along the poolside, and mine on the upper deck, overlooking the ocean. I laid in complete nakedness under my white sheet. I released tension, and a pool of silent tears, on the massage table. As the masseur talked, I subtly tuned him out, aligning my soul with the sound of crashing waves.

It would be my first of two very prominent losses in nine months' time. The past was converging with the present, and my future.

# The Roadie Wife

*Chapter 32*

# MOVING PIECES

    I hit the ground running upon our return from Mexico. Vince and I decided to lease out my condo and move to a beach cottage in Carlsbad, California. If I wasn't busy moving, or working, I was busy planning my third annual Justice Day (the same event where Victoria and I had met Vince and Andrew, three years prior).
    Life had changed so much since the first Justice Day, and I decided that the third annual event would be the *final* Justice Day. Philanthropy had been a joy of mine before Vince, but now with traveling, and the weight of juggling custody with personal time, I was feeling fairly tapped out. With all this, I was very excited to be moving to the beach for some solace.

    We moved in November, and autumn at the beach cottage was wonderful. You could see expansive skies and the Pacific Ocean from the front yard. I enjoyed the morning fog along the coastline. It created that tangible heavy air; the kind so thick it seemed like you could reach out and grab it.

Most people don't even realize living along the coastline is *not* sunshine *all* the time. Many mornings we have what is called, the marine layer; layers of fog along the coastline. Somedays you would need to drive two-miles inland just to catch the sun (this just hit me as an epiphany while writing: sometimes you have to drive through the fog, in an anti-intuitive direction, to find sunshine).

Other days, all I had to do for my unobstructed view of the coastline was to step out my front door and turn right - and then there it was! The great blue Pacific Ocean along Coast Highway. Essentially, I was three doors down from one of the most visited beaches in San Diego County.

Our beach cottage belonged to the family of my friend, Faith. Her grandfather had it since the fifties. Her mother lived there as a girl. Faith, lived there after high school with her mom, and again as an adult with her own husband. It was a sweet cottage with tons of charm.

The only unfortunate part of living in the beach cottage was a new three-story-monstrosity that lined the entire west side. The monstrosity really didn't belong on a 1950's beach cottage street.

Vince and I got to experience the builder of three-story-monstrosity, firsthand. He was a multimillionaire snowbird from Montana and decorated his condo with large gaudy sculptures and chunky wood furniture. His style was quite opposite of our minimalist midcentury modern decor.

The builder rented a small apartment below his condo to make sure the property was occupied when he was in Montana. The tenant was a flight attendant for a small jet stream company. She was easy going and likable, and had a direct view into our dining room from her apartment patio. Thus, *her* patio was *our* view from our dining room.

One day after we first moved in, I had inadvertently left the blinds open overnight on the west side. The next morning, as I was waking up, I happened to be undressed as I walked into the dining room. The flight attendant and I connected eyes and I quickly closed the blinds.

I vacillated between, 'was I rude not to wave?' or 'should I pretend like this didn't happen?' I later chose comedic relief, and introduced myself from the window.

"I'm your new neighbor... the naked one."

"I wasn't going to bring it up." She laughed.

"Well, I wasn't sure if it was more awkward for me or you. I decided me." I grimaced.

"My boyfriend was there with me too on that patio, you know?!' She laughed again.

"Oh crap. No, I did *not* know!" Turning red.

"He didn't see anything though. By the time it registered that you were naked, I turned to tell him, but you had already shut the blinds. Then he didn't believe me." She laughed again.

"There's no faster way of developing an acquaintance than by exposure!" I joked.

We both laughed this time.

# The Roadie Wife

*Chapter 33*

# CHANGING WEATHER

Getting settled into the beach cottage came and went. Justice Day came and went. Vince came and went. And for me, I was in another house, *and* alone yet again. I got out the Kid Rock tour calendar, looking for my next trip (so much for solace).

I was able to find a great opening in Chicago, Illinois when Kid Rock would be performing at the House of Blues in downtown Chicago. My mentor, Cathy, had recently moved from San Diego to the Chicago area: I could see her during my trip to see Vince, *double* bonus.

Vince had off Thanksgiving Day, which meant we could go with Cathy to their quaint family mid-western farm outside the city. It was a great trip with enjoyable autumn weather, a hotel along the waterway in downtown, and yummy Chicago food.

One of the restaurants we visited during our stay in downtown Chicago was along the main drag off the river. We sat in a window booth and watched the people walking by, some doing their Christmas shopping others just out for the holidays. It was glorious. Suddenly, out of nowhere, a man was knocking on the glass from the street at our booth. We both popped back in surprise to a man dressed like Buddy-the-Elf. After he knocked, he began waving and smiling (smiling is his favorite). But, he didn't go away. He just kept waving (long enough that I took a photo). Finally, we decided to wave back (in hopes he would continue on down the street if we humored him). Sure enough, in true Buddy-the-Elf fashion, he continued striding down the sidewalk.

    My trip to Chicago was fun. I was happy to connect with Cathy and enjoy the city. But, as always, the trip went entirely too fast. When I got back home, I noticed Vince would be passing through San Francisco, California near my birthday.

    I don't know about you, but I love San Fran at Christmastime. I don't get excited about Christmas in general, but there is something amazing about riding a trolley down the middle of the shopping district. There are lights sprawled overhead, carolers on corners, people bustling around with arms full of shopping bags and crisp winter air – sans snow. It's cathartic for me.

    I decided to plan another secret-operation-visit. I called Beau to get details on the hotel whereabouts, and made sure he did *not* tell Vince I was coming. I landed at the airport and navigated the subway system to the trolley into the Financial District. I was still a novice with public transportation, but I was improving my skills. I did however end-up a little mixed-up after the subway and trolley, before the City Bus, and decided to hail a taxi for the remainder of the trip to the restaurant.

Beau told me what time they would arrive at dinner, and the restaurant address. I had the taxi drop me a few doors down, in case they were still walking down the street to dinner. I texted Beau to confirm they were inside, and made sure to have Vince face away from the doorway, so I could sneak up from behind. So childish of me, but it was fun because he was not expecting me, especially since we had plans to see each other in Malibu, California in a few days.

It was a fun surprise for my birthday. One of the audio engineers ordered an expensive bottle of wine for me. It was the most expensive wine I'd ever had, or had since, and I enjoyed every last drop.

We had a nice few days in San Francisco. It was during this trip I starting figuring out the crew wasn't so keen on spending time with Kid Rock outside of work. I felt bad for Kid Rock at this point because he was looking for a buddy to go see a movie. I guess he had offered to rent out a movie theatre and take all the crew: everyone declined. But, I guess there is a reason for everything, so I could only shrug.

I watched rehearsals at the vintage club, Bimbos 365, but I left before the show. I took the trolley all the way back to the subway, and the subway to the airport for my flight back home. I closed my eyes on the trolley and took in a deep breath to capitalize, and memorize, the moment, it was bliss.

# The Roadie Wife

*Chapter 34*

# ARRIVING STRESS

Three days after San Francisco I drove up to Malibu, California to the Malibu Inn. The Malibu Inn is a very small venue along the ocean, against the cliffside. Kid Rock usually doesn't play venues that small, but it was a private show. I may have stolen a beer mug from this show…because my beer was in it. My mug made it to the bus, but not back to the venue, and subsequently made it to my house (guilty smile).

During my visit to the bus (where I inadvertently left my beer mug – cough cough), I ran into one of the tour managers. He was exiting the back longue of the crew bus. Behind him was a lady in five-inch heels, mini skirt, and store-bought boobies wearing a shirt with a plummeting neckline. She was adjusting her clothes as she stood up from the lounge couch.

He's married. I know him! This is *not* his bus. That is *not* his wife. This is *definitely* not her bus. I glared at him as he excused himself around me and off the bus. Then, I grimaced as she approached me, still adjusting her clothes, walking down the hall from the back of the bus. What had I interrupted?

These things have a way of ruining my mood, mostly because of my gag-reflex, but also because I would begin imagining what Vince was doing when he wasn't with me.

Through December Vince continued the remainder of the tour and then flew home for a scheduled custody hearing the week before Christmas.

A sarcastic, 'Merry Christmas', to everyone! You get to fight, cry, and spend tons of money tearing your family apart. Who wouldn't want to go through a custody battle?! This proved to be very stressful for me. We had only been married 12 months...officially. I know this train wreck seems obvious in hind-sight, but I hadn't seen it at the time (naïve, or purposefully).

At court Vince's ex-wife pulled me aside to tell me that she wanted her family back, emphasizing how *she* messed up with Vince. She had left him for another man (the man she was living with) and yet she wondered if I could step out of the picture, so they didn't have to 'go through all this'. This wasn't the first time she did something similar to this. But, *this* time I was married to Vince, legally, and wanting to keep it that way. I thought Vince did too, or *at least* he didn't want to be back with her (I guess I could count the latter in my benefit).

I may not have been able to say the same thing regarding David – though I was trying. It was a matter of fact, I had just deleted David's number from my phone. It wasn't the old one I had memorized. He lost that number when I stopped paying the bill for that line. But, he would have random pre-paid wireless phones with a new number every few months. So, it was tougher than you would think to avoid his calls, or even to know if it was him calling. If it was an Oregon number, I knew not to answer it.

I couldn't talk to David about traveling with Vince, custody stress, or my new marriage; those subjects were too emotional. I was still learning to let go of David. There were a lot of moving pieces in this season and I was trying to love *one* man, and completely stop thinking about the other.

I had started getting a lot of calls from David in early spring of 2012. I had answered some of the mystery numbers and we would talk for short stints; it felt like he was doing well. But, there was never a reason for his calls, which made me think, there was a deeper reason for them. It was heartbreaking for me, and those calls seemed to weigh harder on Vince than they had before. Similar to Vince's ex-wife asking me to step aside, it felt like David was doing the same thing to Vince with his random calls.

Kid Rock was doing short stretches of shows in the spring, so Vince was home for a few weeks, and then gone for a few weeks. Vince was struggling with the custody battles and intermittent spring shows. I was invited to the Kid Rock Cruise again in 2012 (a sarcastic, yippy), but I declined, and he had to go without me. Even without the cruise, we both were drinking more. Stress was pulling on every level and we felt stretched at the seams. I was beginning to see a pattern.

# The Roadie Wife

*Chapter 35*

# PERMANENT THINGS

    My first tattoo was to rebel against my parents. In fact, I had planned on getting it on my eighteenth birthday. David talked me out of it that year. I settled for a rebel tongue ring instead. When you get your tongue pierced, you swish around Listerine for three minutes before the tech pierces you. It's the way to numb your tongue in order to push the hollow metal tube through without too much pain. It doesn't sound like that big of deal. But, by sixty seconds I wanted to spit-out the Listerine.

    I sat in the sterile patient chair, closed my eyes, and stuck out my tongue. David and Josh were both watching. I could feel pressure, but no pain. Suddenly, I heard them simultaneously moan 'grosssss' as a piece of my tongue popped out onto a metal tray covered in sterile liner. Then the tech slid the tongue ring into place and screwed it tight. The piercing took less than the three minutes squishing the Listerine.

I was too naïve to know tongue rings had sexual symbolism and was confused when people started asking odd questions about my willingness toward oral sex. I was flabbergasted and I took out my tongue ring within months. The hole closed up within hours.

The following year I did get my first tattoo, alone, in a shabby tattoo parlor. The sign painted on the stucco above the entrance had a dragon surrounding the letters 'TATTOO' in bold text. The shop was crammed between Video Acapulco and Pan Paulita's Bakery. The parlor's front room was about a twelve by eight space, sample artwork on the walls, a flip book on a counter and a half-saloon door leading into the back. It was musty and dark, only allowing natural light from behind the one window covered by wrought iron bars. This wasn't a place I would have visited alone. But, the artist came recommended by a friend with some great tattoos of his own.

I told the old artist, Terry, about how I waited a year for the tattoo, and why I had come alone that day. Everyone I told about my impending tattoo, especially David, told me to wait until I knew exactly what I wanted on my body. I did *not* know what I wanted, but that I wanted one. I didn't have anyone in favor of the idea, so I went alone.

Not having a creative idea of my own, I flipped through some tattoo books and decided on a butterfly. Naively cliché. I decided it should be discrete and picked my lower right back. Unknowingly, cliché again. After my selection, Terry led me in the back through the half-saloon door to his workstation. It had an overhead dentist-looking, double arm-light, that swiveled over the table. I pointed to my lower right side, or my upper-right glute, depending on your perspective. He asked me to lay flat down on my stomach. I had on tight spandex, so he had to yank them down for working space.

"Gotta yank these down a bit." Terry said.

As he pulled my waistline down about an-inch-or-two past *my* canv*ass*. I chuckled because I knew my butt crack was showing and would remain his view, or elbow prop, for the next few hours.

It hurt like a hot poker being rubbed into your skin over and over. The long outline parts hurt a lot more than the fill-coloring. I kept my mind on other things to think through the pain (oh my, another writing epiphany: I would think through my pain, instead of feeling it). Three hours later, my tattoo came out so radiant in coloring that my parents thought it was a fake. Actually, they didn't realize it was legit until months later when it never washed off.

My second tattoo was with David when we lived in Australia. We decided to memorialize our fourteen months in Sydney with permanent body print. We found a little studio in a seedy area, outside Sydney, called Blacktown. I got a fish on my right ankle and he got a tribal insignia on his leg. Both were nonsensical in hindsight and we joked about the ridiculousness of these tattoos for quite some time. But, I guess these moments are how stories are made.

My third tattoo was so underwhelming I barely recall the occasion. I chose another picture from a book (because I had become addicted to body art), in a random studio with David. This time I inked a fairy on my shoulder. I actually like this tattoo, but probably wouldn't have gotten it in retrospect. I hear this is a thing: tattoo addiction. I may have it.

My fourth tattoo was after David and I split up. In fact, I got it to commemorate our divorce. This time, I picked a tattoo from a women's empowering event I had spent months helping coordinate in Sydney. I was more selective with this tattoo because it meant something to me. I would ink: 'Warrior Princess Daughter' text overtop of a sword and princess crown. I laid on my side for four hours while the long sword lines were burned into my skin by an artist who explained how he was just released from prison. I got as far as the sword and the princess crown along my left torso, but then decided against the text.

My fifth tattoo was in the spring of 2012, happenstance, right before my life came crashing down. Vince and I were going through the custody battle with his ex-wife, and I was feeling tattered from it all. So, what should someone (me) do in a time like this?! Yes, you guessed it: I decided some skin permanency would be emboldening. This slogan from Australia would go along my right torso: 'Strong Dignified Honored'.

    I chose a less sketchy artist, and studio, this time. I took Vince with me to About Face Tattoo off Coast Highway. My artist, Jodi, had been in the business for twenty years. He was super relaxed and down to earth. He had never been to prison and wasn't yanking my pants down in a dark room. Jodi worked for two hours pressing ink into my side as I silently repeated the words, 'Strong Dignified Honored'. I wanted this to be my credo, even if it wasn't ringing true in this moment… or in my life.

    'Dignified' seems ironic when referring to a tattoo inked into your skin. But, hey! I never said I was good at picking tattoos… maybe I should stick to writing on paper.

# The Roadie Wife

*Chapter 36*

# JUNE 2012

    Ojai, California holds a Music Festival every year with classical and contemporary music in the Ojai Dome of Libbey Park. If you have ever seen the movie, "Easy A" with Emma Stone, it was filmed in Ojai. It's a beautiful place surround by woods and citrus trees, tucked in the hills outside Los Angeles, where scores of celebrities live. It's small, quiet and quaint.

    Vince's Employer (pimp), Sound Image, held the account for the Ojai annual event and Vince worked it year-after-year. There was a strict no drinking rule in the wooded park, but across from the park was a dive bar, The Hub. In fact, it was the only dive bar in town. Vince and his coworker frequented the bar after rehearsals every evening. One evening in particular, Vince ventured out of, The Hub, into the park with a pint of beer. He called to tell me he was breaking the park rules. He was drunk, I was unhappy and hung up.

    He told me the next day things went from bad to worse as they proceeded to get so blasted they *had* to drive the truck back to the motel together. Meaning, he and his coworker both had to keep their eyes on the road, *and* help each other steer. Moreover, his inebriated coworker decided to skinny dip, under the night sky, in the motel jacuzzi, alone. His coworker never made it *completely* back to his room. He passed out after opening his motel room door. He spent the night on the floor, with his naked butt and legs outside, torso inside.

Apparently neighboring guests did not enjoy the morning view. Vince admitted, although he made it all the way into his room, he fell face first fully clothed, onto the bed without making it any further.

Their company had used this same small-town motel for years. The motel manager warned them both to clean up their act or he'd call their employer. In hearing the stories, my 'unhappy' turned to livid. His reckless behavior could cost their jobs or their lives, or the lives of others.

The ink was still fresh on my new tattoo, 'Strong Dignified Honored', so I mustered my tattoo-inspired ideology and decided that Vince and I needed a face-to-face come-to-Jesus-talk.

The next day was Saturday, so I drove from our beach cottage up to Ojai. Vince was surprised to see me. His happy-to-see-me-smile, quickly turned to sheepish-kid-in-trouble-face. I gave a struggled smile, found a chair and waited for him to finish the set and clean-up for the day.

After his responsibilities were complete, we headed back to the motel. We had a straight, swift talk. I told Vince he had to clean up his act and wasn't sure how much I could tolerate of his carelessness. His drinking was out of control. He needed to deal with his shit or we would be through.

Apparently, I hadn't realized yet, I was *part* of our problem. We were like a snowball headed down a steep mountain. Vince asked if I would stay through Monday so he could drive back with me instead of driving back with the crew. I agreed.

Sunday the crew spent tearing down speakers and cabling intertwined in trees overhead. After they were completely done and trucks were loaded, it was well into evening. I joined them all at a local Japanese restaurant for a "Job well done" sushi dinner.

# The Roadie Wife

*Chapter 37*

# THE ACHE

Dinner was nice, but it was fairly late when we got back to his motel room. I pulled my phone from my purse and saw a missed call. It was Tina Kain, David's mother.

She never called. My heart dropped.

"This can't be good. No Good." I said.

My heart was beating so hard.

"What can't be good? What are you talking about?" Vince asked.

"Tina called. There's a voicemail. Hold on. I need to listen to the message."

I pressed play and walked toward the door, but I never made it outside, the crackling in her voice caused my knees to give-way. I began, what felt like, a slow-motion fall into a seated position on the motel bed. I faced the curtains, staring at the air conditioner knobs, as I listened intently to every broken word.

"Bethany. Honey. I hope you're not alone. Honey. David died last night. Call me back, okay?"

Click.

His passing came as a surprise. Like my own self-fulfilling prophecies bouncing about with Vince and me, David had always said he would die before he turned 33, 'Like Curt Cobain or Jesus Christ – tribute'. He liked to add the word 'tribute' after certain phrases. This statement was one of them.

Had I been waiting for the shoe to drop? Was he trying to contact me because he somehow knew we was going to die? I had been avoiding his calls.

He can't be gone from the earth.

I never said goodbye.

Was this my fault?

*It was surreal.*

I walked outside in shock and called Tina back. She asked me to help her contact people about David's passing. I made a few phone calls right then on the balcony. But, I was shutting down. I got ready for bed in silence. I laid there until I was too tired to think anymore.

The next morning Vince drove home while I made phone calls from the passenger seat. I recall passing through the valley of citrus groves, through Oxnard, and then Los Angeles down the 405 through Orange County. I watched as buildings melded with billboards and cars that we passed. Although I was moving, it felt like I was going in slow motion. Each call was horrible. I sent a text to some people instead. I was functioning without emotion as if it wasn't my story: like I was watching myself from the outside.

The next few days were heart wrenching. I visited Tina on Tuesday. She asked me to help plan the services, and of course I would. She needed to travel to Oregon to identify David's body and clear out his apartment. Brandon and Justin Puda would both help with services too. Vince even helped with some planning and was super gracious during these weeks.

Vince and I had just left our Ojai talk, but those issues quickly went to the back-burner, and faded into the background, as I fell into mourning. Vince was quiet and out of place, but he hung in the backlight of it all. Since, he didn't know what to do with all of it, he just kept moving, something he was good at doing, much like myself.

I had just lost Paisano nine months prior. But I had never lost someone I had loved like David. I had formerly teased Vince that if anything ever happened between him and me, I would always have David. But now David was gone, and more than a backup plan, my heart hadn't learned how to let him go yet; I was being forced into it. What did this mean?

My tears would fall as I passed local spots David and I had frequented. I thought back to our footloose days of dating and being seventeen. I would reminisce of our former, 'happy marriage' days. Sometimes the tears would overtake me in grief. These were dark days for me. Sometimes I would cry so hard I couldn't breathe and my vision would spin out.

I grappled with the fact that all the memories I shared with David were no longer shared with *anyone*. They were *just* mine now... so I was clinging to whatever I could.

My heart was breaking and I wanted God to take me away. I ruminated on the days we tried to make our marriage work and all the sorrowful events during, and after our divorce. I replayed the conversations regarding our attempts to reconcile. I was trying hard to work it all out as I laid in bed listening to John Mayer, "Dreaming with a Broken Heart", on repeat... and David was indeed gone.

*Chapter 38*

# THE BREAK

    Vince and I had been planning a backyard vow exchange for the summertime when our family would be in town. It had been scheduled prior to David's passing, and since our backyard event was only three weeks away, we wouldn't postpone it.

    Family and our closest friends celebrated our vows with a dessert reception under a midsummer ambiance; twinkle lights and the sounds of crashing waves an ear shot away. Of course, it was the third time saying our vows for this marriage, but it was the first time in front of family.

    With David's death in the shadows, the vow exchange was heavy and tear-filled, but refreshingly heartfelt. I was beginning to think this would be my chance to love one man, and *only* one.

    A few days later, Vince was gone, and so was the family who had traveled in for the vow exchange. I was back to work, on a plain summer day in real estate. I was doing busy work when I saw a new email hit my inbox indicating my phone bill was ready to be reviewed and for some reason, this month, I decided to look at it. Maybe, I could scan through and see if I could skim off of ten bucks here or there? Maybe change my phone plan for a better deal? Who knows why I looked at it; it was on autopay.

Much to my surprise, there were more pages to the bill than anticipated. The bill showed a log of every text and every call. It didn't take long before I noticed an unfamiliar phone number with incoming and outgoing texts from midnight until three or four in the morning on Vince's line.

The messages were not to my number! It wasn't my number! Who the hell is this?

**My heart sunk!** The pattern showed night after night. As I delved into more months of past bills, the text exchanges went back for months, and only happened on days I wasn't with him.

I swung around my office chair in one movement and grabbed my phone as I stood and walked to the back exit while dialing Wendy. I made a b-line past my bosses' desk, shaking my phone to indicate I needed to make a call. She glanced up, did a double take, and on her second look, I saw her look of worry and concern. I surmised, by her look, I couldn't hide my own pale face which was covered with a look of panic.

I was hoping to walk around to the front parking lot to sit, but I didn't get that far. I went dizzy and steadied my back against the building. It was 1970's wood siding; it felt like an orange peel. I know, because it was holding me up as I slid down to the curb. It wasn't a cognizant choice, it was a necessary one. I had to sit before the earth pulled me to the ground. Everything began moving...shaking. It's San Diego, July 18, 2012. Before you go running to the earthquake records, it isn't on record because it was happening inside of me.

The curb along the parking lot exit had barely enough space to hold me and if someone was to leave work midday, my feet would be the first thing they would roll over. I was doing everything I could to just breathe while waiting for Wendy to answer her phone.

By the time she picked up, I was shallow breathing, trying to get words out, but they wouldn't come. I just kept breathing to get air to my brain.

"Are you being raped right now?!" She asked worried.

Maybe people call their friends when this is happening, I have no frame of reference for that, but I became worried that if I couldn't get my words out, she might call the police. So, I mustered everything I had.

"I think Vince is cheating on me!" I blurted out.

Back to breathing, head spinning, trying to keep my feet flat on the ground without getting rolled over by a passing car.

"Just keep breathing until you can talk."

She did really great at holding space in that moment, not knowing what was to come next. It had only been a few days since she stood beside me in my backyard as I declared my vows to Vince.

When I could talk, Wendy and I started crafting hypothetical scenarios about what *could* be happening. I asked Wendy where she was, because I wanted to be with her so I could fully process what to do next.

I walked back inside and told my boss I needed to leave early. She didn't ask any questions, which was a blessing for me, as I didn't have any answers. I went back to my desk to shut down my computer and grab my purse. But before shutting down the computer, I did another scroll through the bill, unable to accept any other possible outcome except humiliation. It will be humiliating to announce a divorce mere days after our vow exchange. I was *just* beginning to learn how to love him. Had he started loving someone else?

Wendy is one of my best friends. Born and raised in Orange County, California, she had just moved to Louisiana after my cliffside vows on 10-10-10, but traveled back to California to stand beside me during our most recent vows.

Orange County is a big deal to her heritage. It's a unique area between San Diego and Los Angeles with less pretension than either of its neighboring counties. They are a low-key beach community with old money. A lot of people are attracted to the OC because of popular television shows. But if you are a local, or a native to Orange County, you can spot transplants fairly quickly.

Even though Wendy didn't live in Orange County anymore, she still blended-in like a local. Wendy is a beautiful, middle-aged, fair-skinned freckled woman, standing a few inches shorter than me. She's as straightforward as she is kind, sincere and loyal. Fierce. Unassuming. I was glad to have her on my side.

I got in my car and headed toward the Starbucks off Highway 5 in San Clemente where Wendy was doing her freelance graphic design work (or had been working before I interrupted her day). As I drove, my mind was reeling with possibilities, all of which ended the same way. This was the end for Vince and me.

# The Roadie Wife

*Chapter 39*

# BOTTOM OF THE BARREL

I've read that moments of personal trauma are hard to recall as a personal story. I believe that now. But, I am not sure why some of the moments I can replay in slow motion, similar to when David died. I've tried to recall the drive to Wendy, but I cannot, for the life of me, recall those forty-five-minutes. What had I been thinking? What was I feeling, if anything?

I recall arriving in the lower parking lot. I also remember walking up a bunch of stairs to the coffee shop entrance, which felt like an Olympian task for me in those moments. I recall entering Starbucks and scanning the tops of heads in search for Wendy. I saw plenty of people hunched over computer screens, earbuds in place, some people talking on phones, others texting. I even recall an older gentleman reading a newspaper and thought 'how sweet', a tradition of his generation long forgotten by subsequent ones.

Once I located Wendy, I quickly made my way to her table and sat down at her workspace. Just sitting with her seemed to be a relief. We sat at a round table facing the window out toward the road.

Sitting with Wendy, I know we must have been chatting about all the possibilities, but I don't recall what we said. My mind was in investigation mode, moving through the motions of chatter and conspiracies. My world was falling apart, and I was just trying to keep myself upright.

I kept going back to the bills to find a pattern. He only texted this number while he was touring, and not when he was home with me. I do not know why that relieved me. I can only figure now, after-the-fact, this pattern was a puzzle piece, and I was being rewarded fitting them into place; bringing the picture into clarity.

I decided I needed to call the mystery number that had been texting with Vince. Wendy sat across from me - wide eyed in anticipation.

"You're brave!" She said.

As I saw it, there was no other option.

The phone rang with no answer and I was able to hold back my vomit as the voicemail greeting started. I wanted to hear the voice. I hoped it was a coworker and Vince had only been texting about gig details. But, it wasn't. It was a female... and as I listened, I recognized her voice.

"Oh shit, I know her!" I said to Wendy.

"You do?! Who?" Inquired Wendy

But, ever so quickly went the 'beep' to leave a voicemail and I had to say something.

"This is Bethany Luchetta. Call me back."

I pressed the red button and slammed the phone down on that little café table with eyes of fire! It was Kid Rocks back-up singer!

The singer actually shared Wendy's maiden name, but was of no relation. I told Wendy her name, what she looked like, and my few personal encounters with her. Wendy began Googling her. I could tell by Wendy's expression that sharing the same name with the singer made her a little uneasy. Too close for comfort to share anything with this lady.

My next call was to Vince. His phone also went to voicemail. I left a similar curt message to call me back as soon as humanly possible. Why were neither of them answering their phones? Were they together in that very moment watching my number cross their caller ID? Or worse, what were they doing not to hear their phones ringing?

A thought came to me: Vince was in Minnesota, where his parents had just moved. Kid Rock was doing back-to-back shows in Minneapolis and Vince had planned to visit his parents on a day off. I could call his parents' house and possibly find a puzzle piece to my investigation.

Sure enough, his dad answered the phone.

"Hi, Joe. Is Vince there?" I asked.

"He's out shopping with his mother. Is everything alright?" He asked.

"No. It's not. Please have him call me as soon as possible!" My tense tone was evident.

"Do you need help? Is there anything I can do?" He wanted to know more.

"Is his phone there, by chance?" I had to know.

"Yes, it's here on the charger." He replied.

"Okay. I left him a message, too. But please have him call me as soon as you see him."

"Will do." He finished, in a worried tone, which I didn't try to fix for him.

This information brought another level of clarity to my investigation: *they* weren't together, *ignoring me*.

Less than a month after I had met Vince, I seemingly had to go on a spending spree, holding back restraint, *not* to spend money on traveling to Madison Square Garden in New York City, where Vince was headed for his tour with Jimmy Buffett. He had invited me to tag along, but we had just started dating, and he was in the middle of a divorce (which ultimately didn't slow me down, but I didn't know that at the time).

Believe me, I wanted to go to New York, but I felt it was a bad idea so early in the relationship; too much too soon. I traded the trip for a mini shopping spree and with it, bought the new John Mayer album, Battlefield Studies, with the song, "Heartbreak Warfare." From there, Vince and I had the joke: The Battlefield Studies album cost me a few hundred dollars.

In pondering my costly album (that I still have) and the early days of dating Vince, that was a different type of heart ache which originated from desire and longing: missing each other, wanting to linger every night until the last kiss, hanging in anticipation of when we would see each other again.

But, that new-love-ache was just a foreshadowing of something much more heartbreaking. I was experiencing, yet again, "Heartbreak Warfare".

*Chapter 40*

# PACK IT UP

Faith's family had arranged for us to vacate the beach cottage in August, the month after our vow exchange; they were turning the cottage into a vacation rental. I had begun packing after the vow exchange, for our pending move. So, I was partially packed when finding out about Vince's escapades on the road.

I glanced around the room where I first met my neighbor through the open window and took a deep breath and let out a laugh, which turned into a cry. Oh, how I felt so vulnerable, fully clothed (this time).

This was all so tough.

Packing seemed to provide a sense of control: things fit in their place, a nice square box, taped shut, until I was ready to unpack it.

Sometimes the grief would get the best of me and I would abort packing and head to the coastline and stand against the railing, gazing into the great expanse. I didn't go down to the sand very often during the ten months living there, but I visited the coastline almost every morning, even if to stand there for five minutes and take in the beauty.

Many days I would stand at the railing taking in the changing tide, and crashing waves, and wonder about unpredictability. But some days - just some - the ocean was calm, steady and strong. That's the thing about the ocean: it's so much like life. I could stand at the sideline watching, until I wanted in, if I ever wanted in. Albeit, I would miss something sitting along the side, but I was beginning to think I would be okay missing some things.

I cried myself to sleep almost every night when Vince had been gone since our vow exchange. Without David, coupled with the new discovery of Vince's emotional affair, I prayed several times that I wouldn't wake up the next day. I'd rather go, than stay to deal with it all – to deal with myself.

A few days before Vince's arrival home from tour, I met my pastor at a local coffee shop to help me process my grief. Meeting her at the Old California Coffee House, she sat next to me on the old velvet couch, and with compassion, she let me cry without rescuing me. After listening to me, she said that she had a song she'd like me to hear. It felt like a strange reply to my emotional download, but I obliged. I pulled out my ear buds and plugged them into her phone. She hit play.

It was a new song I hadn't heard, by Bethel Music, "Come to Me". As the song built up dynamics, the interlude bellowed out, "I am your anger, in the wind and the waves..." In that moment, goose bumps rushed down my legs and arms, followed by a tingling sensation from my-head-to-my-toes. My belly lurched, I gasped and let out a deep cry, covering my face with my hands.

Why did the thought of God being in my anger make me feel comfort at a deep cathartic level? Turns out, I mis-heard the lyrics. They actually went, "You are my anchor, in the wind and the waves..." But, I heard what I needed to hear. I heard my whole life that God was my anchor. I wasn't feeling that kind of divine steadiness. I was feeling rage, sorrow, and the depths of grief. I needed to know the God of the Universe knew my anger - like the ocean I had watched daily - He knew my roiling... and my torrid.

In the last days at the beach cottage, it seemed, the coast was the only solace I could find, as I was now seeing God in the sweltering churn of the sea. It was a strange type of solace, but I was glad it was finding me at last.

# The Roadie Wife

## Chapter 41

# HOMECOMING

    It was July 21, 2012 - the last day of the leg Vince's tour in Minot, North Dakota. Vince had decided to finish out the remainder of the Kid Rock tour after my discovery (there were only a few days left anyway). We agreed that was a good choice because I was still grieving and I needed time to process before listening to him. Vince asked if he should find a ride home when he flew home, or if I wanted to get him from the airport. In his prior marriage, his ex-wife often let him find rides home from the airport. I guess that always bothered him, but now I was beginning to wonder why she may have done that.

    Nonetheless, I agreed to get him. I circled the San Diego Airport terminal a few times (I hated waiting in the cell phone lot), checking my texts until I saw, "I'm at the United Terminal curb". I popped the trunk and he tossed his luggage - no welcome home embraces this time. Silently tucked behind the tinted windows, the drive home was quiet. We were both preparing ways to start this conversation, possible requests, replies, boundaries and exit plans.

When Vince left for the road after our vow exchange, everything had been in its place. As I was readying the house for the impending move, I may have placed boxes systematically to watch Vince's face, when he walked through the door, thinking I was moving *him* out. Boxes littered around, as to say, 'someone is moving!' Maybe he would have forgotten for a brief moment we were *both* moving, and I could take pleasure in seeing his stunned face. I didn't get the twisted pleasure though, he didn't react to the boxes at all… more important things on his mind I guess.

We arrived home from the airport and sat across from one another on our overstuffed couch. Soft background music accompanied our conversation, to make it less quiet, and as a witness to our next commitments.
    Would this couch be his bed tonight?
    From now on?
    I needed to see behind his eyes.
    I needed to watch his face.
    Was his reaction sorrowful?
    Did his sorrow hold depth?
    Vince and I had agreed, when we spoke on the phone, he would come home with a proposed plan. I wanted to hear his plan. Would his plan be our demise? I'm familiar with demise, but I wasn't familiar with relational stick-to-itiveness. I did not want to beg him to change. I had begged before, and it hadn't worked. I did however, feel inclined to hear him out.

I had one specific regret with David, one I held tight in the forefront of my mind, when Vince spoke. It was a painful regret, one I didn't want to forget, lest I would repeat it. I kept this memory alive - it was visceral - and still had a heartbeat. I drilled down the memory to the sights and sounds - to the feelings - and let it hang - in suspense - close to my heart as I listened to Vince. I had to do this, it was the only way I was sure not to repeat my pattern:

The memory was from a post-marriage hang-out with David. After we spent time together, I drove home (to my parents), and became more, and more, homesick for David the further I drove from him. I was homesick for us. For the, "David and Bethany" who we had been. My heart broke. It was the chest pain you can actually feel. Tears flowed down my face. My long drive home was in silence while tears soaked my shirt. As I pulled through the hidden gates of the Pauma Valley Country Club, twisting around the golf course, I became dizzy with anxiety. I parked in the driveway, and knew I couldn't bare it anymore. I *needed* David back. I wouldn't survive; I would die of heartbreak.

I dialed David and gathered my composure while the phone rang. He answered and started small talk about how I had just left his house.

I interrupted. I had a bad habit of interrupting.

"What are we doing?!" I cried.

"Talking." In his sarcastic tone.

"Why aren't we together? Why? Can we just go back in time and start again?" ***I begged***.

"Ummm..." Silence fell on his end of the line.

I imagined his girlfriend had arrived to visit after I left, or that his roommates, the Puda Brothers, were standing nearby, David shifting away as to block any volume coming from the receiver.

"I. Am. Sorry. I'm sorry I've hurt you. I'm sorry I let you go. I pushed you away because I was afraid of getting hurt. But, now *this* hurts. I'm sorry I stopped caring *and* got distracted *and* forgot about **us**. Let's try again. We both just need to change!"

I started bawling and became less coherent.

"We know that won't work." He said kindly.

"Why? Please. Please. Let's just try. Why can't we just try? I. Am. Begging. You!" I said with emphasis.

"Let's talk another time." He became quiet.

"Fine. Understood." I hung up and tucked away my vulnerability with my hard reply... *and* there, I left it. I had hung up just as impulsively as I called.

Still in the driveway, I hung my arms over the steering wheel, hands dangling overtop, head dropped between ten & two, sobbing until I couldn't catch my breath: pure defeat. I used my sleeve to absorb the snot and tears until my sleeves were soaked. The moments were consumed with survival while hyperventilating for air.

My heart was shattered and I didn't know where to start in order to find the pieces. Dazed for oxygen, I sat alone in the dimming light, gazing into the darkness of my soul, where I couldn't locate what I was searching for. My begging had failed.

Regret became my cruel lesson that day – severe but fair. I had danced around the edges of my marriage with David. We had let our eyes wander away, and our hearts too. I had begged for him back, but it was too late.

# The Roadie Wife

*Chapter 42*

# THE PROPOSAL

The regret story with David was the moment propped up in the corner of my mind on the couch with Vince. The memory was standing steadily: Do not wall-up with Vince. Do not be rash.

I didn't want to learn from regret again - not if it depended on me.

I was ready to hear him out. Vince opened his journal and began to read me some notes. He had a few days to thoroughly process what proposed next-steps he would offer for our relationship. I listened as he listed off suggestions. I peered over to see his journal notes aside some bullet points:

- Quit touring with Kid Rock.
- Work only local shows.
- Start making friends.
- Therapy.

He had already left a message for our pastor, the same one who witnessed our most recent back-yard vow exchange, to meet for clergy advice. He was also looking for a therapist to work on *why* he felt inclined to become comfortable with Miss-Back-Up-Singer, and other women who gave him attention, out on the road.

    I felt a peace come over me in a calm wave, settling me into the couch. The feeling was out of place for the moment, yet I gladly accepted it. Was this denial, or did I subconsciously know he was a good man? Did he have hidden festering hurt, like I did? I needed help too, and didn't know which way was up. I didn't want to throw away another marriage to find myself in the same lurch as I had with David. I feared becoming a calloused-witch-man-hater (which I was totally capable of becoming at this point).
    As Vince and I sat, I agreed his list sounded like a plan. I admitted we both needed help healing from our old junk left unkempt. We sat quietly and my ears caught the background music of Matt Kearny. "All I Need" was playing. Every time I hear this song, I remember this moment of decision: to face our pain.

> *I guess we both know we're in over our heads.*
> *We got nowhere to go and no home that's left.*
> *The Water is rising on a river turning red.*
> *We all might be okay, or we might be dead.*
>
> *Everything we got is slipping away,*
> *I meant what I said when I said to my dying day.*
> *Holding on to you, holding onto me.*
> *Baby it's all gone black but you're all I see.*
> *You're all I see.*

As crocodile tears flooded out the brim of my saturated eyes - **this was my moment** - I had to reckon with it. Even though we were treading water, we were losing energy going down fast. We just had to acknowledge it and find a life preserver.

Decisions had to be made. A direction had to be chosen. I'll never forget this night with Vince. Never. We didn't say much more. There wasn't much to say. Actions had to play out.

It was late and he had traveled all day. We went through our bedtime routine in a reverent silence. I was surprised by my desire to hold him close.

Hadn't he just torn my heart apart?

Was this just grief?

I wanted him to caress me.

Maybe this is a thing: a need to solidify love after trauma? I had been lonely. But loneliness wasn't a stranger to me.

We slid into bed and like magnets and embraced. Tears were in both of our eyes. We slowly made memorable love, as we never had before.

# The Roadie Wife

*Chapter* 43

# RECKONING

Trauma unravels in strange ways. I wanted to keep my eyes open. I was beginning to feel like I had shut them somewhere along the way and I couldn't see what was right in front of me all along.

The new song by NeedtoBreathe became my mantra, "Keep Your Eyes Open". The name of the album with the song, reinforced the season I was passing through, *The Reckoning*.

That is what I was doing: reckoning.

For all intents and purposes, Vince had quit touring. He had told his boss in San Diego that he wasn't going on the road anymore, and he even told him why. The last part impressed me. He had just been promoted to Monitor Engineer months prior when Beau left the tour for another gig. Vince had worked up to this promotion for four years. He was excelling at his job, and Kid Rock liked how Vince ran the stage. It was the most income Vince had ever made, and this position could take him to great new heights in the industry.

But, instead he had to quit, and before he could, he had one last gig in Toronto, Canada. It was for a festival which Vince had already committed to work. He would also use that gig to inform Kid Rock, in person, he was no longer be his Monitor Engineer.

Vince asked me to travel to Toronto with him. He would have to see, Miss-Back-Up-Singer and wanted to be as transparent with me, as he possibly could. I asked him to call her before we left and to be *very* clear with her about ending all communications. Then, I asked if I could be on the line, to make sure she knew, that I knew, and that we all agreed on the severity of the subject. I now admire my courage to insist on this in the midst of my delirium. I must've wanted to push every ounce of questionability out of the realm of possibility.

The phone dialed, and I was sitting across from Vince. She picked up. He explained that I was sitting there and their communication, and time spent together, had been inappropriate for two married people. She sounded defensive and began to back track that she wasn't doing anything wrong. Vince insisted it had to end. She finally agreed and I closed the conversation by curtly thanking her for ceasing all communications with Vince.

August tenth we would fly to Detroit, and go onto Toronto from there. Tour management had already purchased airline tickets for the crew, so I had to buy a solo ticket. It wasn't cheap, the flight was full, and the airline couldn't put our seats together. The airline attendant at the terminal explained, once on board we would have to ask passengers to trade seats with us, if we wanted to sit together. Onboard, we tried to arrange our seating, but we couldn't find a solo traveler to swap seats with. I shrugged, "par-for-the-course". We were to sit apart for the length of the flight.

The ladies next to me brought their dog on board. I'm fairly sure dogs are meant to stay in their under-the-seat dog carrier. But, these ladies started drinking, and then got their dog out of the carrier, passing him back-and-forth from lap-to-lap, and proceeded to serve him whiskey from a mini bottle.

I was in a bad place emotionally, but this drunk dog / drunk lady situation, made me feel worse. I was in the window seat, feeling very stuck: stuck in many ways. I pressed my face against the window, turning from everything, and let my tears fall.

# The Roadie Wife

*Chapter* 44

# TORONTO

    Landing in Detroit, Vince would meet the tour bus because the crew, and band, had to drive across the border into Canada together because of customs: everyone had to be accounted for on their passenger record into Toronto. Therefore, I couldn't tag along in the bus, I was neither crew nor band.
    We deplaned into the terminal to see my flight on the screen into Toronto was DELAYED in red. Vince grimaced knowing he was the only reason I was there. He was already feeling bad about us spending extra 'insurance' money for me to come along, then the ladies with the dog, now a delayed flight, and he had to leave for his bus pronto.
    We said our goodbyes and I settled into a corner near my gate in the empty terminal to wait. I was alone with my thoughts, pondering what I would do when I saw Miss-Back-Up-Singer.
    How would I feel?
    Was I prepared for this?
    I could feel the anxiety rising in my chest.

Four hours later, I finally boarded, and took the quick international flight into Toronto. Landing, I called around for a taxi to the festival venue and began to realize how far the venue was by the responses from the taxi operators.

They didn't go that far? After a few calls, it was recommended I call a car service. I had never used a car service before (this was pre-Uber and pre-Lyft days), but located some in a directory. I chose best price for the distance: an *hour* drive! As I waited for "my car" I was stunned when a black limo pulled up. I shook my head in disbelief, and a little embarrassment. Now wishing I had arranged a rental car; *this* surprise car trip was definitely nothing like the surprise car trip Victoria and I had back in Ohio with the Mercedes rental.

I guess the bright side was having a limo helped through security. I arrived at the venue and got through into the bus bays with very little effort. I found Vince's bus, unlocked the bus door with the combo code, and made my way up the stairs inside.

Vince was up on side stage, so I chatted with some of the crew before they escorted me to the stage. Vince was hanging out enjoying some of the acts before Kid Rock performed. The stage was erected in a grass field: Boots and Hearts Tire Motorsports Park, Oshawa, Canada, Ontario. Kid Rock was the headliner and was meant to make a spectacular arrival on a helicopter. Something about descending on rope.

I hung out side stage with Vince and we watched Phil Vasser, who I had seen before in San Diego, with a guy I had dated a few years prior. We also saw the old band, Alabama. I had listened to them when I was young. Their music was still good, but their plastic surgery was *not*. It wasn't long before it began to rain, and then rain harder. I don't know how Canadians party, but they didn't seem to mind the rain.

Vince and I got some dinner in crew catering backstage and relaxed under the big tents while the rain was coming down. We caught up with some of the other crew guys, and band members, during dinner. We joked a little, and I was reminded of the day I met Mark: "Never swipe! You never swipe!"

They were all bummed to see Vince leave, yet none of them knew why. I surmised they must have thought I pulled some roadie wife ultimatum – but I hadn't. I wanted to throw Vince under the bus when a crew member was trying to tell me, "this roadie life is tough, but if you could manage to give it more time, things would be okay". Talk about laugh-out-loud!

It was time for Kid Rock to make his appearance. Luckily, the rain had subsided. When walking back to stage, I got an alert on my phone, my data was approaching limits for out of the country usage: my phone would be shut off when I reached my data limit. Shit... I had forgotten about getting an international plan for this leg of the trip.

We made our way to side-stage to see fireworks, strobe lights, confetti, and a half Canadian, half American flag rolled-down for the stage back-drop.

Moments later, Kid Rock descended. I looked across the stage and felt my stomach surge. I saw her face. I heard her voice. I watched as she danced... and swung her hips... and snapped her fingers. I couldn't fake "okay" in this moment. I wouldn't be okay. I did my best for a few songs before tapping Vince on the shoulder to say I was headed back to the bus.

Alone on the bus, I sat in the driver's seat, this time I dialed Victoria. My phone alerted me again, nearing data shut off. Victoria picked up and I began to wail. I'm not really sure what I said. I was dizzy. I had snot all over my face, and then all over my hands from wiping my nose. I was blubbering. She was offering compassion and reassurance when the phone finally shut off. It helped to hear her voice, even if just for a brief moment. I moved to the bunk and finished crying it out on my own. The rest of the trip was a blur.

I got back to San Diego and started grief counseling for David's death. I also hired a Classical Homeopathic Practitioner to delve into some newly surfacing health issues. Vince and I were scheduled to meet with our Pastor. And Vince had found a therapist, for marriage counseling, and solo counseling.

Thankfully the therapist referral was a good one. We *both* liked him. Without knowing about our recent Canadian trip, the therapist used an expression toward Vince in our first session: re-gaining trust would be like walking to Canada.

Mic-drop! Thankfully it was only an expression, because I didn't want to go back there anytime soon.

*Chapter* 45

# FINDING SUPPORT

My parents happened to be moving to Hawaii the week we got back from Canada. We helped as much as we could, but we were moving from the beach cottage that week too. I decided not to tell my parents anything about Vince and me, except he was hoping to go back to college to change careers.

Vince decided he would enroll in community college because if he couldn't tour, he wanted another career. He would still have to work for Sound Image in the meantime, but he would work locally in their shop. We took a huge financial loss when he quit touring. He could cover child support and medical coverage, but I had to swing all the other bills.

Vince's birthday was approaching at the end of August and I had planned to go see Cathy, my mentor, outside of Chicago on a solo trip so I could process all the aforementioned. Vince hadn't planned to be off tour during his birthday, so he wasn't coming with me to Chicago. I would be gone for his birthday, so he went ahead and planned solo trip of his own: backpacking in Idyllwild, California.

I spent a lot of time with Cathy unpacking what had happened with David, the struggles of being a stepmom, and what was happening with Vince. Cathy was the safest person I knew, and I confided in her how I felt unmotivated to continue living while lost in confusion.

Cathy held space for me in this time with understanding, wisdom and compassion. For the first time since sitting with my pastor at coffee, I didn't have to play pretend.

Then it came time to update my bosses. There were only three of us in the office: me, my boss and my other boss (they were married and owned the company together). Like most small offices, your work / personal life had less distinction. I felt it was only fair to keep them in the loop on my ever-changing personal life.

My boss was a predictable guy. So predictable, I could predict his response to the news about Vince. The three of us sat in the back of my office, my boss in his chair and his wife next to him. I began to tell them what events had unfolded. I explained to them my plans for moving forward with Vince: get healthy myself, and allow Vince to figure out his own stuff.

"I've seen this before Bethany," my boss continued, "...a spouse cheats, and the other one thinks things will change. But they never do."

"I can't say I disagree. But I have to give myself the chance to get healthy. And I might as well allow him the same grace." I said.

I knew the statistics. After all, my first marriage had failed, and so had Vince's, both for similar reasons. I guess deep inside I was hoping for more support from my boss, even knowing his predictability.

"We are here for you, we can help in whatever way you need to make this easier on you." She said.

She was kind, knowing the pain she had seen on my face a few weeks prior. We all left the conversation open-ended, agreeing that I would keep them updated.

If I had known how intense my summer was going to be, I would have never committed to the Tri Rock Race in San Diego with my older sister, Heather. We had been training for the swim, bike, run mini race for the better part of the year. I didn't want to tell Heather about any of the stuff with Vince because I was ashamed. So, I did my best to stuff-it, and keep moving. But, admittedly, my "moving" wasn't too enthusiastic.

The morning of the race had a slight chill as we set up in the staging area along the bay. The chill would burn off quickly, so we soaked up the cool, knowing soon we would be sweating under the sun. I did fairly well on the swim portion. Heather and I finished that leg of the race together.

I passed her on the bike portion though. I loved biking the most, but Heather wasn't as skilled on a bike. I have a vague memory of her helmet sitting too high on her head because it was borrowed, as was her bike (it was too small for her also). My recollection was something like an adult riding a kid's tricycle, knees smacking at her chin, although I don't think it actually looked that bad. Ending the bike portion ahead of her, I dismounted and took off my helmet and headed for the track. I knew Heather would undoubtedly pass me on the run.

At the 4.0-kilometer mark of the 5k, I wanted to toss in the towel. I just couldn't do it. I was mentally and emotionally spent. My legs didn't want to move anymore. In this race, you couldn't wear earbuds because there are pedestrians everywhere in the village, and racers needed to stay alert. But, I was not alert. I was lost in my thoughts, and they began pulling me down like weights.

It was in that moment I understood why people use race metaphors for life.

Another fellow racer came alongside me. A stranger. She began to encourage me to finish the race. She started talking to me as if she saw my thoughts. Maybe I was talking aloud and hadn't realized it? But, she had energy. Stamina. She had hope to finish.

"Let's do this. We can finish this!" She said.

I felt like she was a trainer or something. I wasn't even sure if she was talking to me...or someone else.

"Hi." I replied.

With shortness of breath and uncertainty, I looked around to see if she was *indeed* talking to me. She saw my race bib and continued her statement.

"You're in... my category. Women... 30-and-up. At our age... we can do this. We only need to... take one step...at a time." She believed.

She broke up each fragment between her breaths while running.

I thought she may have only been in my imagination, so I repeated back to myself silently, "one step at a time". But, I didn't even see the finish line, so maybe instead of one-step-at-a-time, I should just sit down.

She continued to coach me between breaths.

"Not much... further now. We came... all this way. We can cross... that line. We will be... proud we did! Can you feel it?! We can... do it! One step... at a time. I am going to... finish this race... with you. I won't let you quit." She reinforced.

She was so encouraging and I felt like her light came to surrounded me angelically. I was overcome with emotion and gained a burst of energy to keep going (even if just to make her proud). She ran alongside me.

A stranger.

Like she knew me and my story.

Before I knew it, we were coming down the final stretch lined with photographers and cheering crowds. Passing under the finish banner, I looked over to thank her, but she had disappeared into the hordes of family and friends. I slowed to my finish and was decorated with my Tri-Rock lanyard.

I never saw her again. Had she been a delusion?

She was right though, I had to keep going.
Just one step at a time.

# The Roadie Wife

*Chapter 46*

# HAWAII

    The first week of October Vince worked the Believe Cancer Walk in Redlands, California. It was a long workday for him with set-up at two in the morning, for their five o'clock kick-off. After the race, crew tore down gear and Vince and I headed west, toward Hollywood, California.

    We had promised Naomi and Michael Chislett that we would help them move their belongings to storage and clear out their condo. They were moving back to Sydney.

    Vince was exhausted by the time we arrived in Hollywood. But like a champ, Vince kept his word to help move. We made trips back-and-forth to storage (and to the dumpster) all afternoon. We finished packing the remainder of personal belongings, and then Naomi cooked us a nice vegan dinner. We soaked in our time with Michael and Naomi. All-the-while, Vince and I kept an unspoken agreement that "everything was fine" with us. Façade in full effect.

Three days later, we left for our anniversary trip to Hawaii. Vince had wanted to volunteer in the annual Kona Iron Man Triathlon his whole adult life, so months before, we decided Hawaii would be fun for our anniversary and Vince could finally work the Triathlon.

Vince used to participate in triathlons, bicycle races, and high school track & field. He recounted the memory to me of the days in his living room, when he would remove his bicycle tire, set his bike on blocks, face the television, and pedal along, stationary, with the annual Iron Man Triathlon. He is still an avid bike rider and in great physical condition. If he had the time and sponsorships, would probably enter an Iron Man Triathlon himself.

He almost took this anniversary trip alone. I considered it bittersweet celebrating a second wedding anniversary with grief and betrayal looming just under the surface. But, I thought: Vince would be working the triathlon, airline tickets were purchased, and I had a beach front condo reserved. So, I threw caution to the wind and went along for the ride. I also went along pretending things were okay between us, and decided against telling my family in Hawaii about my crisis with Vince. My little sister, April, lived in Hawaii, and my parents just moved near April's family, so I opted for the smokescreen.

The majority of the trip was fairly uneventful. I spent most of my time at our beach front condo, journaling on the balcony, with my clear water view. The afternoon before we left, Vince had some spare time and he wanted me to go snorkeling with him. The problem is, I don't like going in the ocean. Strike that: I am terrified of the ocean. I hate the waves and I hate that unknown creatures are swimming beneath me.

I politely declined the invite, but I agreed to go watch from a safe distance. However, once I was down on the white sand, the warm clear blue water seemed like a dream. It was nothing like the murky beaches in San Diego. I decided to wade into the water a little. Vince pointed out all the colorful fish passing by our feet. It felt like I was in an aquarium. My curiosity got the best of me and I deicide I would put my face into the water with the mask and snorkel.

The water stayed fairly shallow for a good distance, then coral reefs began to appear below me. I knew enough not to put my feet down, so a slight panic came over me. It felt like I was in a glass coffin, but I kept breathing and tried to focus on the brightly colored fish swimming around me.

I was beginning to feel confident in the water, as Vince motioned to me, while pointing toward the coral. He found a treasure!? So, I swam toward him to see what he had found. Just then an eel was winding his way from the coral toward me. I flew back in maximum terror. Flailing arms to get away, water came in from the top of my snorkel and I swam up to the surface to rip-off my mask for air.

Catching my breath, I heard the sounds of yelling from the shore and saw the lifeguard was waving for us to move out of the surf. I looked the other direction, into the surf, in time to see oncoming surfers. My eyes widened at the surfboards coming directly at me.

My immediate reaction was to put my feet down and dash away, but as I did, I brushed the reef, being reminded that I *couldn't* put my feet down.

I did my best to swim away from the boards while coughing up water, but I choked on more water as the waves came at my face. I was caught in a current.

Vince is a strong swimmer, and an excellent surfer, so he made it through the current with no issue. He figured I had been tailing behind him, and was already halfway back to shore, when he turned back to see I was still out struggling in the surf.

"Swim to shore." He hollered

I wanted to yell back, 'No shit Sherlock!'. But, yelling wouldn't help. I was stuck with the eel *and* coral reef below me, the surfers coming toward me, and my inability to swim in the current. I snapped back to my hatred for the ocean and began to cry. I know I looked pathetic.

The lifeguard, who hadn't taken his eyes off me, mounted his board and headed for a rescue. The whole beach began standing, hands on their foreheads to block the sun, in order to get a better look at the event... and I was the event. But, I didn't care. I cared more about being saved from my "current" predicament than I was about the show... or my tears.

"Not from here, are you?" The lifeguard said.

He approached, belly down on his board, paddling along with his arms.

"How'd you guess?" I retorted sarcastically

"The current gets pretty strong right here, all the locals know that. You weren't paying attention as you were drifting." Answering me.

Not in the least bothered by my teary sarcasm, he slid off the board and told me to grab on. I pulled my torso up onto his board, butt hanging off the side, and he pushed me back to shore.

As the water got shallow, I stood up and thanked him. He nodded, tucked his board under one arm and headed back to his post. The onlookers went about their business too.

Vince headed toward me smiling ear-to-ear, as if he was watching a comedy unfold, I scowled at him in return. I started walking, but instead of stopping when I got to him, I passed right by him, slamming my mask and snorkel into the sand at his feet. Without a word, I headed back to the vacation rental and the tears rolled down my cheeks leaving him to collect all our things on the other side of the beach.

# The Roadie Wife

*Chapter 47*

# MEMORY LANE

My younger sister, April, had lived in Hawaii for about six years. As I walked alone back to the condo, the reel played back to all my shitty trips to Hawaii. Maybe Hawaii isn't the place for me, I thought. Ruminating on these memories during my walk back to the beach front condo, made the walk more exhausting, but I couldn't help the train of thought.

"I drowned my sorrow in tropical alcohol back then, I guess I can just do that again." I said aloud.

My prior visit to Hawaii was just months after I met Vince. My family in California all decided to venture to April's house in Kona for a family reunion. My family was in a strange place of disconnection (we more-or-less have always been that way). But the disconnect seemed more heightened during that trip. We were all together in paradise, but it didn't feel like paradise. It felt like, "together-alone", much like my childhood had seemed.

To pass the time on that trip, I spent a lot of time calling and texting Vince. I hoped it would help me feel connected to something. Admittedly, *my* behavior and attitude, did *not* help with the disconnection between the family on that trip.

That trip with my family somehow poured salt in my singleness wound. I was the only one not married. I didn't have any children. I was over thirty, and I *wasn't* feeling fabulous. I felt like *all* I had were my wasted years.

I rented a moped, and cruised the coastline, alone. I read books, drank and played games. I did what I could to keep my mind distracted.

It was the Saturday evening of my family trip, when mom asked April and I if we would go to church with her on Sunday. I was indecisive. I didn't want to think about God. I probably should have answered her honestly. But instead I conceded to go, reluctantly.

The next morning, we were dragging to keep our commitment to her. As time started slipping with readying the kids, my mom became increasingly disappointed and frustrated. Saying things like: "If you don't want to go, fine!" "I want you to go, but don't do it for me." "I really just wanted us to be at church together." and "It will be good for the kids." I could be released from obligation, but not without guilt.

So, finally, we piled into the van and got on our way. As my mom studied the clock on the dash, she muttered something about getting there before the music was over.

I sat in the front seat of the van. April was trapped in the back behind car seats with the kids. I guess I had enough of *something*, because I became increasingly aggravated. So, what was I to do at a time like this? You got it: I picked a fight by questioning the importance of church. At least that's what I remember.

"Then, you should have said no!" My mom said.

Touché. But, I didn't let it go.

"I didn't want to deal with your backlash if I declined, so I grudgingly said yes." I snapped back.

April was stuck in the back of the minivan, wide eyed and quiet.

"If you don't want to go, then just get out!" My mom exclaimed.

The gavel hit the block! And so, as the van slowed to a stop sign along Ali'i Drive, I opened the door, while the van was still moving, unbuckled while grabbing my purse, and was out of the van before she came to a full stop.

I could see my mom's jaw drop, in my peripheral, as she watched me walk away from her... and the van. Cars began to honk for her to go, jolting her back to reality. She continued through the stop sign, but moments later she circled around, slowly passing me while asking me to get in the van.

"You better hurry or you will miss the music!" I said sarcastically.

I dashed across the road toward a book store.

They never made it to church that morning. I got settled in the book store and dialed Vince to tell him of my woeful story. Then I waited for April to give me a ride back to the house.

When I got back, it was icy quiet. I built my wall a little higher. It just reinforced my self-fulfilling prophesy of being alone and unwanted. Self-pity was my only companion at this point; the payoff was isolation. I can't say I hated being alone with my sorrow. What I didn't know was: sorrow doesn't easily relent once you let her be your buddy. And my buddy, I had made her.

*Chapter 48*

# OCTOBER 2012

    The next day after the eel incident, Vince and I headed back to the airport from our short anniversary trip in "paradise". Driving along Ali'i Drive I was swept away with another movie reel from my first Hawaiian trip.

    My divorce had just been finalized with David and I needed an escape. Hawaii happened to be a good place for getaway, and I could visit my little sister. This memory caused me to feel despair. I would never forget how many times I questioned David if we were making the right choice with divorce. But, David always told me that divorcing was the right thing for us, and after-a-while, I believed him.

    The day I was leaving for my first Hawaii trip, David called to question *me* this time. I had pulled up to a stop light, flipped on my blinker, heading south for the airport, my phone rang and I picked up.

    "Are we making the right choice?" David asked.

    He had never talked like this before. I had become so calloused from begging *him* to come back. I was feeling spiteful *he* was asking this question now.

"Yes, you will see. Just like you always say. We are doing the right thing." I answered candidly.

"Maybe we aren't." His confusion was evident.

"Look, I am headed out of town to Hawaii right now. I can't talk about this. I am trying to put it behind me. We have done the right thing. We already tried to make it work. Remember?!" I was curt and harsh.

I wasn't sure if I heard crackling in his voice, the traffic, or my blinker, as I waited for the cars in front of me to make the turn. I couldn't handle any of it: the blinker needed to stop and I needed to hang up the phone.

"Okay. Bye." Sorrow pulling back his voice.

"Bye." I hung up.

My heart was beating so fast. I won't ever forget that moment. It was one of two times David had called in the slightest remorse of what we had done to each other.

Even though he always said splitting up was the right thing, it felt like an ugly mistruth. It was a lie we both bought, and resold, in defense of our pride.

Could I just ignore what had happened with Vince and Miss-Back-Up-Singer? My last time in Hawaii, I was falling in love with Vince. Now I was second guessing my decision to marry again. Moving away or moving toward, which was I doing? One thing was for sure, I was spinning my wheels. There were dot's, but I wasn't connecting them (not yet anyway).

Will I let Vince go?
Would Vince be added to my list of regrets?
Could I love Vince from a safe distance?
Was this part of the problem?
I wanted to keep the good and banish the bad.

Vince and I arrived at the Kona Airport and were waiting in the pseudo-terminal under a tiki-style hut in their open-air pavilion for the flight back to California. It was slightly humid with tropical rain streaks in the distance, which was common every afternoon on that side of the Island. My phone rang, so I stepped away from tiki-terminal and answered.

"Hello, it's Bethany." I said.

"Hello it's Doctor Chan from North County Women's Specialties." She continued, "We would like you to make an appointment with your primary care physician. Your blood test shows positive ANA results indicating you are struggling with a form of Lupus. It's an autoimmune disease and you will need further evaluation. I am glad we did the tests so you can get some help."

"Um, okay. I will call my doctor. Thanks for calling." I said, a little cluelessly.

"No problem. Sorry it wasn't better news. Have a good day." And she hung up.

I hadn't actually known what Lupus was, or an autoimmune disease for that matter. I would soon be arms deep in research about the nature of these diseases and how they take root inside a person, more specifically me.

Back in September, I had my annual check-up and my regular OBGYN doctor said I had appeared especially depressed. I told her it felt worse than depression. She was concerned. I rambled a long list of the same symptoms I had told my homeopathic practitioner and she suggested that I have my blood checked to rule out vitamin deficiencies, or "anything else".

She indicated that if nothing was unusual with my results, I should consider anti-depressants. She ordered a battery of tests and I went to the lab. Her call, with the results, came to confirm what I was feeling; my body was fighting itself from the inside out.

I gave Vince the news from Dr. Chan and we sat in the tiki-terminal chatting about what may be next for my health.

Our plane ended up being late out of Hawaii, making us late for our connecting flight in San Jose, California. It caused us to miss the last flight to San Diego.

Once we arrived in San Jose, the airport was closing down for the night. We called some local hotels to grab a room, but there was a convention in town and everything was booked. I looked around and saw other groups of unlucky travelers getting settled in for the night. I scrunched my nose, and sighed deeply, knowing my fate for the evening.

Vince and I looked for a mildly secluded place to get comfortable on the airport floor. One perk, we traveled with back packs instead of luggage. We tucked our bags between us, and under our heads and tried to rest, emotionally and physically.

Airports are noisy (even when they are closed), so we didn't get much sleep, and by the early hours of the morning, my hip bones were sore from the hard floor. I sat on the flight back home to San Diego contemplating my summer - death, betrayal and loss of self. I thought back to all the pride I took in being one of those independent, stable types, who could pair well with the roadie life, "even if I wanted a man, I didn't need one".

Now, I wasn't sure if it was the reality of my sore, aching bones from the airport floor, or **pure certainty** of the fragility of life, but I was becoming resolutely determined to give myself a chance. And if I needed a chance, Vince probably did too.

*To Be Continued...*

# The Roadie Wife

# Special Thanks

Thank you to my adoring husband, without your tenacity, my **next** book would have a different beginning.

Thank you to Cathy Hartley for your unending love, you are my tangible version of Jesus incarnate.

My number one cheerleader, Livvy Lou, because of you, I have seen miracles. You are a gift.

My remarkable graphic designer, Wendy. The book is awesome because of the cover! You are dear to my heart.

Victoria, you were always there to cry (and eat) with while these stories were being created in real time. I love you.

Jana Hoppe for being an amazing editor... and friend.

Michael Chislett, for friendship of 20 years, and counting!

To Dawson Daugherty! I've loved watching you grow into a man of your own musical legitimacy. Keep walkin the line.

To 5 Two Press for believing my series will produce much going forward.

Jeannette Smith for making the book smooth in new ways.

Finally, the lover of my soul, Jesus Christ, for without Your sacrifice, my life would mean nothing.

"Bethany is to be commended for publicly baring her soul in order to show others that sex is the sharpest of two-edged swords...pro-life and anti-life, definitely not a toy!"

**William Barkley**
*Bethany Luchetta's Grandfather*

"To love at all is to be vulnerable. Love anything and your heart will be wrung and possibly broken. If you want to make sure of keeping it intact you must give it to no one, not even an animal. Wrap it carefully round with hobbies and little luxuries; avoid all entanglements. Lock it up safe in the casket or coffin of your selfishness. But in that casket, safe, dark, motionless, airless, it will change. It will not be broken; it will become unbreakable, impenetrable, irredeemable. To love is to be vulnerable."

**C.S. Lewis**
*The Four Loves*

CPSIA information can be obtained
at www.ICGtesting.com
Printed in the USA
JSHW050038140123
36072JS00006BA/130